CONFESSIONS OF A VICAR'S WIFE

D1388826

Other books by Jane Grayshon

A Pathway Through Pain (Kingsway, 1987)
A Harvest From Pain (Kingsway, 1989)
In Times of Pain (Lion Publishing, 1989)
Faith in Flames (Hodder and Stoughton, 1990)

Confessions
of a
Vicar's Wife

JANE GRAYSHON

MITRE
TUNBRIDGE WELLS

First published 1992
Reprinted 1992
Reprinted 1993

ISBN 1-85424-154-0

Produced by Bookprint Creative Services
P.O. Box 827, BN23 6NX, England for
Mitre an imprint of Monarch Publications
P.O. Box 163, Tunbridge Wells, Kent, TN3 0NZ
Printed in Great Britain

Contents

To the vicar's wife's husband:
best friend and lover

INTRODUCTION

I did not set out to write this book. I rarely admit to being a vicar's wife, never mind having the fact displayed on the front cover of a book. These confessions evolved, on radio.

I was in the studios of BBC Radio Merseyside one Friday with our team of presenters preparing, as usual, for the Sunday morning programme. The producer was away and somehow the atmosphere seemed ripe for a bit of a joke.

Next door Elizabeth, another member of the production team, was speaking into the microphone; Peter was recording her report while I awaited my turn. Through the soundproof glass Elizabeth was unable to hear our comments, although we could hear her on the speakers. The two of us shook our heads grimly. Most unusually, her report was awful. She had begun to sound pious.

Suddenly Peter moved.

'Quick!' he said, wheeling his chair backwards from the control panel. 'Let's fade in some really dirge-like music before she finishes her last sentence.' He leapt up and strode over to an untidy shelf.

'She'll have to rerecord anyway,' he said, as if excusing himself, while he flicked through the records and scanned the lists of possible sound-effects. 'But this would be a more inventive way of letting her know the truth.'

He grabbed an LP and pulled it out. 'Here, one of these...' He threw me the sleeve while he pushed the record onto the turntable. In his haste he put on the nearest track to the needle.

Suddenly, blaring through the speakers of both studios, were the famous Loony Tunes, dancing in carefree abandon. The music was in ridiculous contrast to Elizabeth's report; it spoke of fun and frivolity and life.

That did it. Immediately I knew: that is how I would like to present the supposedly pious Christian life (which is how people imagine life in a vicarage in particular). Using the Loony Tunes as the theme tune, I could envisage a whole series on radio telling what life is really like: not pious and funereal, but fun and full of sparkle.

I spoke to the producer. As ever, he was game for anything (well, almost anything). In the New Year we began.

My aim each week was to give a tiny reflection of the Incarnation. The what? you may ask. Exactly! People often do not understand the big words of church. They don't understand God. They understand normal, everyday life. So my aim is to share how God himself is reflected in our everyday life – and everyday jokes. Because, contrary to the image in some people's minds, God is not stuck in church. He became one of us. And some parables and miracles give a strong hint that Jesus enjoyed a great sense of humour.

The series took off. Letters began to trickle in at first, but more than that were the comments passed. Wives told me how they would give their husbands a poke whenever I was saying something which men ought to know about women. Men were chuckling, occasionally bristling, at the cheek of what I had said. Alarms were set for 8.25 on Sunday mornings to wake people for the loony vicar's wife (or rather, the loony wife of the nice vicar).

Several reports came in of people meeting on their way to church and their conversation being orientated around what 'she' had had to say on that morning. Consistently, letters and telephone calls were asking: is this vicar's wife real or fiction? And local bookshops told me their customers wanted to know if they could buy the book of her confessions.

Now you can. And if you have any consideration for the finances of a vicar's wife, you will refuse to lend this book to friends. You will send them out to buy their own copy.

I cannot take any credit for this book without acknowledging the rapport and support from the whole team on that Radio Merseyside programme, and especially the producer, Graham Carter. But the broadcasts would not have continued without the encouragement of so many listeners. And, of course, I would have had no source material without my friends who happen to be parishioners; nor, indeed, without my husband who happens to be a vicar.

1

Stay Pure!
(or, How *int*eresting!)

7th January

I *never* introduce myself as a vicar's wife. It's a conversation stopper. I can be having a rare old time with other people when suddenly someone will shout across the room, 'Oh, chatting up the *vicar's* wife, are you?' Immediately a silence will descend, and whoever had been chatting to me will eye me as if to say, 'Where's your twin set and pearls, dear?' Then they will either apologise for any flowery language they may previously have uttered, or they'll smile politely, tilting their head to one side and saying, 'How *int*eresting!'

But the rapidly-appearing glazed look in their eyes gives away the fact that they're not interested at all. It's as if a shutter has come down. I can almost see their mind whirring away with a terrified, 'Agggh, she must be unbearably holy! How can I get away?'

It's infuriating! In fact, if I want to have any relaxed, sociable conversation on such occasions I'm forced to leave out the fact that I'm a vicar's wife.

Last Sunday evening, New Year's Eve, Matthew and I

were at a party in bonny Scotland. We normally spend a few days with our friends around Hogmanay. We both feel especially at home with them as they have known us since school days: hence they see us as 'old friends from school days' rather than 'vicar and vicar's wife'. There is no need to be on our guard with them.

At about half-past midnight, in the middle of dancing the Gay Gordons on the front lawn (we were all quite mad), I found myself having a conversation with a stranger about vasectomies.

I had introduced myself as a research midwife, you see, and my partner had politely asked more about the research. Quite naturally my answer included the vasectomy bit. It transpired that he was due to have one, and he was really worried about it, poor man. The least I could do was to reassure him that it wouldn't be so awful. And I knew it was not taboo because at one point I even saw his wife glance across to me as if to say, 'You tell him! Please!'

Anyway, there I was telling this strange man all about the unkind cut when a deep voice behind me boomed, 'Stay pure! Stay pure!' I turned round just in time to see someone I didn't recognise pointing to me, shaking his head as if in warning to the vasectomy man, and mouthing, 'She's a vicar's wife.'

Well, that was it. The poor man blushed to the roots of his hair and beat a hasty retreat, stuttering profuse apologies. I felt even more sorry for him than I had earlier. It seemed a most insensitive interruption.

Why do people think that vicars' wives are so pure? And that that purity has nothing to do with practical living? I presume he thought that we're angelic – not defiled by worldly talk. Normal talk.

But that's just it, you see. We're normal: normal people. It just happens that the teacher I married is now working full time trying to share God's love with other people in whatever situation they're in. Which is the same as any other Christian; the only difference being that my husband works at it full time.

And because people come to the vicarage with such a variety of enquiries, I have to be quite unshockable. My past experience as a nurse and midwife comes in very handy. The infertility clinics were especially relevant preparation. They taught me to listen out for some of the roundabout ways in which people talk.

I'll explain what I mean about that next week.

Visitors
2 (or, Yes Please, I'd Love a Sherry)

14th January

You know the language estate agents use? The way they say things like, 'House with ample scope for development,' meaning, 'It's a total and absolute shambles.' It's a bit like that living in a vicarage.

For instance, on Tuesday this week, Marmaduke arrived. (No, Marmaduke is not his real name, but when I gave him the choice of pseudonym that's what he suggested.)

As he stood on the doorstep he announced, 'I'm returning some things you left in my car last week.'

Now, one might have thought that he was simply returning some lost property. But no, because this was the first time in his life that he had come *without* being invited. And although Marmaduke may be one of the cleverest, most highly qualified professionals in the whole church, there are times when even he is unable to explain the confusion of fears and feelings within him.

By the time he'd downed a cuppa we realised that his greeting on the doorstep could have been interpreted

something like: 'My wife's just announced she's going to chuck in her job and I don't know what I think about that, but if I'm going to dissuade her I'll have to be quick before she acts; and I don't know what to say, if indeed I should say anything at all; and do you think God says anything to humans in this sort of situation?'

Thursday brought another coded message. Gerty was full of cheerful smiles when she told us she was 'just popping in – haven't seen you for ages'. She was too shy – by which I mean she didn't feel her needs were important enough compared to ours – to say directly, 'Jane, I'm feeling absolutely ghastly. My mum's had a stroke; I'm exhausted visiting her in hospital every day, and I'm wrung out emotionally... and, yes please, I'd love a sherry.'

Sherry-drinkers are more expensive than tea- and coffee-drinkers.

Telephone calls are different. They don't need quite so much interpretation. Some of them are pretty direct... like one when I was in bed asleep.

'Where's the vicar? Has he forgotten?'

That's all she said.

I asked who it was, and then, still having no clue as to what Matthew had supposedly forgotten, I said I was very sorry but Matthew was out.

'Well, we're all sitting here...' she launched off again.

I wanted to say, 'Well, I'm asleep here!' Or even, 'Hello! Hello, this is me. *Jane*. You can use my name if you like. I don't keep my husband's diary, and he doesn't go through his diary itemising every minute of his day to me. Does your husband do that with you?'

At times I need God to help me to love people. Even to want to love them.

Do I disillusion you, sounding so aggressive for a vicar's wife? I'm not very nice – I know. I confessed that to Violet on Monday. Now Violet I can talk to.

Don't say it! 'Vicars' wives aren't supposed to have special friends in the parish.' It's well known and the advice was repeated to me very clearly several times while Matthew was still a curate. But Violet's so homely and kind. I can cry with her as easily as I can have a good laugh. So when she came on Monday evening, I told her how down I was.

You see, over the Christmas holidays I noticed how really grouchy I can be. I am worse when I'm ill, or when I'm having to take strong pain-killers. But that can become an excuse, can't it? So my New Year resolution this year was to ask God to do something about it ... well, me.

It turned out that Violet feels exactly the same about herself. We prayed together, asking that God would rule our impulsive thoughts.

People might think I'm pleasant. They might think vicars' wives always are. But they see us at our best. Underneath we're the same as everyone else, with rotten stinking resentments about people being rude on the telephone.

As Violet left I asked, 'Will you remember to ask me if I'm *allowing* God to change me?' Because that's part of it. She'll have to remind me – even nag me. So she'll have to be brave – even Violet is still a little bit in awe of the vicar's wife.

But I hope she does. That's what a real friend would do, and we all need them.

3 No Conceptions at the Vicarage, Please!

21st January

I must say, the *food* was delicious; at the clergy party, this is. Beef stroganoff, a superb casserole of turkey in cream sauce, chilli, lasagne, salads... And if your vicar stinks of garlic at church today, I can tell you now, it'll be from Friday's garlic bread. It was wicked – but wonderful.

The conversation was another matter altogether.

I suppose it was bound to be a bit guarded since we don't know one another that well. We rarely meet. I rarely meet my own husband, come to that.

One vicar was trying to sell rabbits. Rabbits? you may ask. The story was that a family had split up before Christmas and there had been nowhere for these two rabbits to go, so someone had dumped the hutch at the vicarage (where else?). There were now seven rabbits. Hastily the vicar's wife concluded the explanation: 'The female must have been pregnant before they came to the vicarage, of course.'

'Why "of course"?' I wondered aloud. 'Couldn't she have *got* pregnant at a vicarage?'

We're such a mixture of people. Someone from the other side of the Pennines (and she begged to remain anonymous) vowed she would *never* go to one of these clergy get-togethers again.

'Last time I went,' she said, 'the conversation was deadly. And no wine was allowed, of course.'

'No wine?' I interrupted her.

'Ooh, no,' her voice reflected a communal shocked disapproval of the very mention. 'We're all supposed to be in awe of one minister who's tee-total. No one dares to question his decrees.'

I did propose that, if she could muster the courage, she could go again taking a bottle with her. She could present it with an innocent smile, offering this as her contribution to the evening. But then she's more gentle and tactful than I am, so she'd never do that. However, I noted that she enjoyed thinking about it.

But Friday. The evening was redeemed for me when I met Charlotte, who was a hoot. She regaled me with stories from their time when her husband was a curate in the south of England. Like the day when the bishop and his wife had made a special visit to their home. In the middle of lunch, her three-year-old had asked the bishop's wife if she had a pattern on her unmentionable underwear. Charlotte had wanted the floor to swallow her up. Apparently, the bishop's wife hadn't batted an eyelid and had given a most gracious and honest answer.

Charlotte went on to recall a time when she and a friend sent out official-looking letters to other curates, fresh from theological college. They had managed to get hold of some headed notepaper and typed a letter to each curate saying that the college was sorry but it was short of one essay, so could the curate now write 10,000 words? They chose ghastly subjects.

Perhaps it was the atmosphere of Friday evening, but there was a definite spark of mischief and suddenly our imaginations took flight. Together we came up with a brilliant idea which we felt sure would brighten up the rather solid-looking bunch present.

There's a hospital in London which exists specifically for clergy and their families. We wondered if we could get hold of some headed notepaper from there and write to some vicars we know.

You can guess the first operation I thought of.

We could put, 'Thank you for your enquiry about your operation. We are pleased to inform you that a bed is now available for you...'

The possibilities are endless.

4 Taking Barbara Cartland's Advice

28th January

There is one thing I do do that's pretty vicar's wife-ish. I'm on a Diocesan Committee called the Houses and Glebes Committee. It sorts out all the clergy housing (or tries to).

Actually, I'd never admit it publicly – to them – but I quite enjoy those meetings. At least, I enjoy the possibility of being just a little provocative. Just a touch, of course. Because it happens that I'm the only woman on a committee of about thirty clergymen.

At my first meeting the surveyor showed us plans for a new vicarage. He pointed to the study and he had the cheek to describe it as 'the working area of the house'! Nobody else noticed, but *I* gave a sharp, audible intake of breath. However, he couldn't have understood my hint, because he repeated the same mistake on the next vicarage. By that time I'd plucked up a bit of courage and I suggested to Mr Chairman that the working area of any house should refer to the kitchen.

They all smiled as if I'd made a good joke. Huh!

Thereafter they tried extra hard to demonstrate how unchauvinistic they were. On the next house it was emphasised that the kitchen window should not face the brick wall of the church (perish the thought!) but should have a brighter outlook onto the garden. One man, directing a big beam in my direction, said, 'It would be much nicer for Mrs Whatever-her-name-was, to have a pleasant view as she peels the potatoes and does the dishes.'

I said, 'It'd be very nice for *Mr* Whatever-his-name-was, while *he* peels the potatoes and does the dishes....'

However, I think I spoiled the piercing effect of my words when the chairman saw the mischievous twinkle in my eye. I'm beginning to see that the Bible's command for husbands to 'love their wives' is much harder for them to obey than most of us wives imagine.

For one meeting I had a terrible panic that I might not arrive on time. I felt it would be a disgrace to walk in late, yet I had only twenty minutes to do a twenty-minute car journey *and* park *and* get to the boardroom. (It's all terribly official – men in suits around a posh boardroom table. I'd never been to a board meeting before.)

I had twenty minutes to do all that, but in addition I hadn't put on any make-up. It's not that I always wear make up, but I do pride my position as the only woman, and I have to represent the female gender well. A bit of colour, a bit of light relief, is always welcome in among boring dark suits.

And I often remember what Barbara Cartland once said. If the chips are down and there's some absolute emergency which forces a woman to choose only one thing to wear – either mascara or knickers – her advice was, *always* choose the mascara.

I was fully dressed but I challenged myself to achieve both. I dived into the car, drove at about ninety miles per hour into Chester and, whenever the traffic lights were red, instead of cursing I pulled out the mascara and ladled some on.

I was telling myself that I was doing brilliantly when suddenly, out of the corner of one eye, I became aware of the car in the lane next to me. The driver – a man – was watching me in fascination. No doubt the unexpected entertainment relieved his boredom as he waited in the queue.

I felt myself blushing immediately. Fervently I began to pray that this man was not going to the Houses and Glebes Committee meeting....

5 Hello Dahling. Can't You Sleep?

4th February

A vicarage telephone hardly ever stops ringing. Mostly, that's great. I take it as a compliment that at last, after we've lived in this parish for five years, folk around us see us as talkable-to people. They phone us simply to be friendly. I would hate to think that friends would distance us from themselves simply because they think we have our heads in the clouds.

Occasionally, people we don't know will surprise us by phoning about important events in their lives. It seems, in a peculiar way, that speaking to the vicar is a way of saying that they want God to be involved in those events too. That's exciting for us to see.

But sometimes, when the telephone rings on and on, time after time, I confess it seems to take over. The problem is that family life continues at my end of the telephone while they're speaking. And I don't seem to have the knack of juggling both efficiently.

I have tried. For example, once it was my editor who caught me immediately after I'd spent an hour answering the wretched thing receiving parish business calls. I felt a bit more like the vicar's secretary than his wife. And then there was the editorial director no less, who wanted me.

'I wanted to talk about your manuscript,' he said. (I sensed that this would be the kind of talk which would make me feel good; appreciated.) 'Is it a convenient moment?'

'Fine, fine,' I lied, shutting the door behind any noise the children might make.

It was only about two minutes later when my dear daughter Philippa let me down completely. It took her two words: 'I'm finished!'

I had an urgent desire to ignore such a call but Philippa's shout echoed around the loo walls even more loudly the next time.

'I'm *fin-ished Mum-my*!'

Sigh! So much for me trying to put across a professional image. One day I might be brave enough to ask people — even people who give my ego a boost — to call back at a better moment. They say honesty pays off.

But *does* it, I ask myself?

Rachel, the minister's wife near here, seems to get away with anything. She's mastered the enviable skill of efficient bluffing. She has lengthy chats with people without even knowing who it is at the other end of the phone!

Mind you, I don't envy some of the awkward situations in which she lands herself during the process. She confided to me recently that occasionally she finds herself chatting to people face to face, on her very doorstep, thinking to herself, 'Now, who is this person? *Should* I know their name?

At least I am honest enough to remain blank and gormless until I know who I'm speaking to. At least, I am usually. Just once — and only once — I let the side

down completely. It wasn't so long ago: around Christmas time. Quarter to midnight. As my brother Pete and his wife had left our house only about ten minutes earlier, I was sure this would be them announcing their arrival home and continuing the frivolities of our evening. So I lifted the telephone with the words, 'Go on then....'

There was a pause.

I should explain that Pete is a whizz-kid drama teacher; he often uses silence for effect. So I determined that I wouldn't let him fool me this time; I'd thwart his supposedly dramatic pause.

Mimicking a strong Dame Edna type accent I said, 'Hello dahling. Can't you sleep?'

Whoops. It wasn't Pete. It was someone called Billy, who was upset. There was a row going on in his house and Billy had thought the vicar might help. I apologised as best I could.

Thankfully Billy was very forgiving towards me. In fact, I'm relieved to say, I spoke to him recently and he doesn't bear a grudge at all.

Come to think of it, we could do with more folk like Billy in our churches.

6 Oh God, You're Norr, Are Yer?

11th February

The trouble with being a vicar, or his wife, is that people make certain assumptions about you and they cannot cope with changing them.

Let me give you a really good illustration.

Several years ago we had a student to stay with us called Gary. He was a down-to-earth, cockney chap; no messing. He liked a simple life.

One evening Matthew made the meal. (You can tell this was years ago.) He really went to town getting everything just so. He concocted a delicious Cordon Bleu rag-out of rabbit.

'Mmmm,' said Gary, halfway through his huge plateful, 'this is really nice, Maffew.' He couldn't even wait to empty his mouth before speaking. 'I really like chicken.'

'Good,' said Matthew. 'Though to be precise, Gary, it's not chicken. It's rabbit.'

Gary stopped in mid-chew. He put his knife and fork straight down, put his hand up to his mouth and seemed to struggle hard to swallow even that amount.

'But I don't like rabbit!' he moaned.

Matthew and I both chuckled at the joke. It wasn't until he refused to eat one more mouthful that we began to realise that he couldn't see the contradiction. Gary was really prepared to trust his assumption that he disliked rabbit more than the evidence that he had already relished half a plateful.

The same principle applies with Matthew's job. People can be completely relaxed and at ease with us when they think they are talking to friends. But at the first mention of Matthew's job, they suddenly seem to withdraw like a frightened tortoise. It even affects my friendships with other mums in the school playground.

One morning last week a steady drizzle began to fall as I was dropping the children off at school. Seeing Anne waiting at the bus stop, I stopped to offer her a lift. She thanked me and said, 'It's dead nice of you to give me a ride in your car. I didn't want to get me hair all in a mess. I've got someone from Liverpool coming round for coffee.' She dropped her voice to a confidential whisper. 'She's a minister's wife.'

I suppose I should have made it my business to confess then that I'm one too. But I didn't have the heart. Anne was nervous enough at the mere thought of one coming later; it might have finished her off to learn that she meets one every day outside school.

Also, perhaps a bit of me sensed that she might say more; she might talk about 'them' as if I was on her side. Such a prospect appealed to my nosiness. What *do* people say to one another about vicars' wives? And so, ignoring the prickling feeling that I was being very naughty, I said nothing.

Sure enough, Anne went on, 'I've hoovered the house and done all me dusting ready for 'er.'

Goodness me, I thought. Do people go to such trouble for me?

We reached her house and the dreariness of the sky had reached our spirits. 'Won't ya come in for a quick cuppa to cheer ourselves up?' she urged.

Soon we were both standing in her kitchen with a mug each. She pointed to her best china. 'I've got the tray all ready over here,' she said.

I don't think she expected me to be impressed – only surprised, with her, that a minister's wife should come round to her house. Or maybe she wanted a little sympathy: she was still terribly nervous.

'You have to do that for a minister's wife, don't you?' she said, enquiringly.

If I said nothing, I reasoned, and she had later found out, she would have considered me terribly odd.

I said, 'I think ministers' wives are equally happy with a mug in the kitchen, if not happier. In fact,' and I knew my voice was sounding very quiet, for I really didn't want her to hear me, 'I appreciate being treated as a normal friend instead of the fuss which I get from people who know I'm a vicar's wife.'

She blushed to the roots of her hair.

'Oh God, you're norr, are yer?' she said. 'To think, I've always thought of you as just Jane.'

I watched her face carefully. I hoped that in her mind she wouldn't suddenly place me in a glass-fronted display cabinet along with her special china; along, no doubt, with where she kept God safely tucked away. I didn't know how to tell her I didn't want special cups, or special talk; simply her friendship. But something about her blushing discomfort made me fear that I had been categorised: 'Different.'

As I drained my coffee, I felt for those few minutes as if I shared how God might feel when the door is closed to keep him out of everyday life.

7 St Valentine

18th February

I don't know if some people think vicars' wives aren't supposed to get Valentine's Day cards, but judging by the looks Matthew got when he bought mine last week, I guess so.

Mind you, he did rather ask for it.

He had gone to a fairly classy shop – maybe that was to compensate for his guilt at having forgotten Valentine's Day two years running. But classy or not, it was still a scramble with loads of men pushing to reach the last cards on the shelf.

Having decided on the card he thought suitably romantic for me, Matthew came across another which immediately made him think of Gerty's daughter, Rebecca. She's young – sweet seventeen – and just starting to go out with her first serious boyfriend. All is going well – *except* she doesn't dare tell her parents because he is much older than she is. She fears their disapproval.

So when Matthew caught sight of a card saying something like 'To my youthful Valentine' he thought to himself, 'That would break the ice.' He imagined a few questions being planted in Gerty's mind if a Valentine card landed on their doormat. 'That might help them to realise she's growing up.' Vicars do try to do helpful things.

So he joined the queue to pay, clasping one card for me and one for Beccy. The chap waiting in front of him was sighing impatiently, and at Matthew's arrival he turned a little – you know the way you stare vacantly around for lack of anything else to do as you wait. He looked at Matthew's two cards and gave a jovial but knowing wink. Matthew, feeling pleased with his choice, smiled in reply, but was surprised that the fellowship in a shop queue should allow the other man to enter so enthusiastically into the spirit of his joke.

It wasn't until the lady serving him joined in the quizzical looks that he thought any more about it.

'You do want – both – of these?' she asked.

'Please,' he nodded innocently.

It must have been the suppressed smirk on her face which gave him the clue, for then, suddenly, he twigged. Of course! They had both assumed he must be having an affair.

Her eyes lingered on his dog collar. He'd forgotten he was wearing it.

Both of them were trying, by now, to conceal their amusement at their different private jokes. The more she fumbled for his change, the more Matthew enjoyed imagining her conclusions.

She must have thought he was an idiot not to conduct himself more discreetly. Fancy being so obvious as to buy two cards simultaneously!

Maybe she'll contact a Sunday newspaper with the scandal. 'VICAR'S SECRET SEX LIFE: NEWS-AGENT TELLS ALL.'

If she wants a witness, I think I might be able to

provide one for her. There was a lady last Sunday when we were out for lunch, and she didn't know me at all. She noticed me when Matthew came up to where I was sitting comfortably on the sofa, and as he bent down to me he rested his hand on my knee. That particular lady next to me nearly fell off her seat! She clearly thought the vicar was frightfully forward.

Scandals are so innocently begun.

8   Beersheba

25th February

Last Sunday made me feel on top of the world. Nothing fancy: I'd gone to Beersheba, the second church where Matthew is vicar. I only go there about once a month, but because they hadn't seen me for a while, they were extra warm. They quite made my day. It is amazing, the power of ordinary people being really nice.

One lady, Mildred, took my hand and gave it a squeeze. 'I listened to you this morning on the radio,' she said. Her eyes sparkled warmly. 'Aah, it's lovely to hear you.'

The lady next to her agreed. 'I set my alarm specially for you,' she said.

Then Herbert joined in. At least, he walked past, muttering and mumbling as if to himself, but clearly for us to overhear. His humour consists almost entirely of dry asides while he's on his way somewhere else. Even on his way to or from the communion rail he'll stop beside a pew and exclaim, 'Cheer up, me duck!' or, 'Freezing in this place, it is. I feel as if

I'm having me body cooled in the mortuary afore me time.'

Last Sunday, though, the cold church was not the subject of his comments.

'Enjoyed waking up to you this morning, Jane,' he said.

I smiled appreciatively but he, pretending to ignore my response, kept his face straight as a poker. He turned to the other ladies and gave a wicked wink.

'There's nothing quite like lying in bed of a morning, and hearing the gentle tones of the vicar's wife while I wake up.'

Had Herbert been forty years younger I think I might have blushed.

But the ladies chuckled merrily. There's a great spirit at that church. Everyone is so very open with each other, with no beating about the bush. If they don't like something, they say so. (Especially about the vicar.)

All the ladies are called Mildred, or so it seems. Rachel, the minister's wife in this Ecumenical church, had the most awful problems in her first year here. Whoever telephoned her always said, 'Hello, Rachel, this is Mildred speaking.' Rachel was too polite ever to say, 'Yes, but excuse me, *which* Mildred?' She had distinct problems if they asked her to get her husband to phone them back.

Another lovely thing about Beersheba is that a few folk come along who, because they've stayed as children mentally, always join in with everything a few seconds behind everyone else. Hence, the congregation's 'Amen' is followed by a second, very loud, 'Amen' from the third row. Saying the Lord's Prayer together can be very confusing.

But they are very special: as God's own children. A few weeks ago one of them – another Mildred – led the prayers. The minister stood next to her and, after a rather extended time of proudly beaming around at everyone, she eventually began. Frequently she stumbled, and she had to be helped over several words. But she persevered.

The moment she'd finished, and before her friend had said her own 'Amen', she ran clumsily and noisily back to her seat. Her eyes were alight, and through the silence when she had jumped onto her seat, everyone heard her exclaim excitedly, 'I did it!'

What she had done was far more than she would ever know. She had allowed us all to see the pleasure in doing something for God. She had shown us that even if the only thing we can offer is a really poor, faltering attempt, God never despises us.

I wonder how many people will follow her footsteps; will stand up in front of others and make their own offering before God.

9   A Most Unholy Row

4th March

OK, so don't tell everyone, but we had a row last week. And when I say a row, I mean a row with a capital R. Our third in fourteen years of marriage.

The confusing part about it was that we were both enjoying a very creative week. Each of us felt fulfilled working hard at what we believed God wanted us to be doing. There was no reason for us to get so angry. Ugh, that old devil does get in to destroy what is good. He is even referred to as the destroyer who 'prowls around like a roaring lion, seeking whom he may devour'. Well, roaring lions must have seemed tame compared to either Matthew or myself.

I'm not going to tell you what it was about (apart from anything else, you might take Matthew's side), but I will say that I didn't know who to turn to or where to go.

Because it got to the point where I slammed out of the door for a walk. I had to get out of the house. I suppose that must have been partly for effect but unfortunately

Matthew didn't even look worried. Indeed he called after me, 'I hope you feel better after the walk.'

Huh! That made it much worse. Maybe I would have felt better if he hadn't sounded so obnoxiously rational. As it was, the whole effect of my storming out on him was ruined by the fact that I then felt guilty. And jealous of a man's objectivity.

So there I was, tears streaming down my face, walking down the road. Where was I going? I had no idea at all. All I knew was that every time I saw anyone else walking along the road I dived down a turning to go a different way. It was awful. 'Fancy being in such a stew,' I muttered, despising myself.

I passed the neighbours' houses thinking, 'They'd be so shocked if I called: the vicar's wife getting peeved with the vicar! They wouldn't know what to say to me. They would just gossip in the school playground tomorrow.' Fat lot of use that would have been.

Outside Gill's house I hesitated. She had come to me often enough and fired off about men. But I didn't just want a moan. I wanted to trust whoever I spoke to: trust them to treat me as a person, Jane, and not the wretched vicar's wife. Yeah, that's the phrase, too: wretched vicar's wife.

Violet would be out on shift work. And I couldn't go and tell Rachel: she would never succumb to the distressed state I was in. In any case, her husband the minister was too gentle ever to speak crossly to her as Matthew had spoken to me.

The only person I could have gone to was Marmaduke's wife, Mabel. She knows what it's like to be Somebody's wife, a VIP's wife, being expected to be perfect all the time... and disappointing them.

But her house is two or three miles away and I didn't have the energy to walk that far.

Eventually I came to a stream in a little valley where I

stood and had a howl. But I was soon interrupted when I saw a couple approaching. They might have thought I'd been attacked by a bad man or something and they might have offered to help. (Maybe I had been! Maybe I should have accepted their help?)

Then it started to snow. That made me feel better, because I hoped Matthew would feel guilty for the fact that I was out.

He didn't. When I got back he said, 'Hard luck getting caught in the snowstorm.' No sympathy. No apology for his contribution to the foul atmosphere which had driven me out in the first place. It was as if he thought the whole argument was mutual. Which, most irritatingly, was probably correct. We had both – vicar included – got our relationship all wrong.

It took us all evening to get round to being warm to one another. And I shall not pretend that we'll live happily ever after without any repetitions of such a row. But I will tell you one thing. The following day, very hesitantly because I was pretty ashamed of myself, I told Rachel what had happened.

She breathed a huge sigh of relief. 'At last,' she confided, 'I'll feel able to come to you now when I walk out in a huff!'

10   Badges

11th March

I was all ready to tell you about the new vicarage doorbells today but that will have to wait. I'm absolutely at
screaming point about being referred to as the vicar's
wife *all* the time. It's as if people think that's the only
thing to say about me. Grrrrr!

Last Tuesday took the biscuit. I had been invited to
speak to a group of students on the subject of pain. As
the students tumbled into the room, the tutor crept
across to the platform where I was arranging my lecture
notes. His kind, welcoming gestures were a prelude to
the question on his mind.

'Jane,' he said gently, 'how would you like me to introduce you?'

'As Jane Grayshon, please,' I answered simply, without looking up.

He paused, hovering beside me. Clearly he wanted
me to say more.

I carried on sorting my reference books into piles,
mentioning as I did so my nursing background, my

research into pain... and when I saw him still waiting for me to say more, I suggested he should say as much as he felt appropriate about my experience of pain.

I think it's quite reasonable to assume that that is far more relevant to a bunch of medical students than the fact that I'm a vicar's wife. But did he think so? Did he!

A little smile was forming on his face – just enough to make me think, 'Uh-oh, here we go.'

He picked his words so carefully, as if the wording made things any better. 'How about saying your husband is a vicar?' he ventured at last.

I didn't answer him directly. I looked him straight in the eye and asked him, 'Forgive me asking this, but are you married?'

'Yes,' he shifted uncomfortably, 'and I'm often introduced as being married when I give a talk.' He blinked hard as if in preparation for some sort of attack.

'OK, OK,' I reassured him, trying to temper my tone. 'What does your wife do?'

'She's a secretary.'

'Right. Have you ever been introduced as a secretary's husband?'

Immediately he threw his head back with an infectious, bubbling laugh. I found myself joining in, despite my offence that he was merely categorising my question as a joke. However, I think he got the point.

Anyway, the matter has all been put into its rightful perspective. All is well with the world again today. God has had his very own way of restoring my equilibrium. I do enjoy his sense of humour.

On Wednesday I went with Matthew to a huge convention of Christian booksellers where there were five or six hundred delegates. Several of them knew me. They knew me *not* because I'm a vicar's wife, but because I'm an author. I even had a badge to say so.

Actually we had a few jokes over those badges. Like

one lady I saw. Now, what I didn't know was that she was a newspaper reporter. So I nearly choked on my coffee when I read her badge. It just said, PRESS.

'Oooh,' I said. 'You should be careful where you pin that label.'

Fortunately she took the joke in kind, and, after giving a furtive glance around she moved it down from her – well you know where people always pin their name badges – and she put it safely. Right in the middle of her tummy.

The next lady wasn't much better. Hers read, PAT.

As for the person whose huge badge right across her bosom said simply, EXHIBITOR ... Matthew and I had difficulty containing ourselves.

I'm digressing. My badge said my name and, AUTHOR.

People kept recognising me and they came up to say hello to me. Indeed, they not only spoke to me, but to Matthew as well. They'd say to him with huge respect, 'Excuse me, are you – Jane Grayshon's husband?'

Matthew thought this was absolutely great. He positively glowed. In fact, I noticed that he got much more pleasure and prestige from being an author's husband than I do from being a vicar's wife.

Whatever way round you play it, men always seem to win. It's not fair!

11   Meetings and Doorbells

18th March

In vicarages right across the country, the vicar's wife is often regarded more as a function than as a person. One of her duties is to act as receptionist, opening the front door of her own home to people who do not want to see her at all.

The time has come for us to take action.

The issue becomes a problem whenever there is a parish meeting *chez nous*. This is a pretty regular occurrence, sometimes with twenty or more people.

Matthew's meetings usually contain great hilarity. In fact, I positively miss out, not just on sitting comfortably in my own sitting room, but on good fun.

I get to deal with the chores instead.

For a start there's always some keenie who comes far too early. They usually catch me bathing the children. In fact once, when I had hopped into the bath with the children, Dan arrived, unknown to me. He shouted some joking comment up to me from downstairs and, thinking he was Matthew, I thought

of a reply and opened the bathroom door to deliver it....

Anyway. The big meetings. The trouble is that there's a span of about twenty minutes while everyone arrives. During that time the doorbell rings almost non-stop, time after time after time.

Knowing that my husband is just as capable as I am of getting up from his comfortable chair to open the door, I usually disappear. I like to give an opportunity for him to prove how liberated he is.

Unfortunately, though, I cannot get too rigid about that. For example, let's say his meeting is in full swing and the doorbell rings. And say Matthew interrupts his meeting to go and answer the door, only to find one of my cronies on the doorstep 'just dropping round for a natter with Jane'! That wouldn't be very good. That would be evidence of the vicar's wife positively hindering her husband's important work.

Mind you, that can work two ways. *I* can be in the middle of composing some brilliantly descriptive piece of writing and I can be disturbed by the doorbell, only to find someone wanting the vicar. Nobody complains then, do they, that the vicar is stopping an author's important work? Interrupting my flow and they don't even want me...

So – wait for it – we've decided what to do. We have rigged up two doorbells. There's one (which goes drrring) for those who want to see the vicar, as if it's his office; and there's a different one (which goes ding dong) for those who are calling to see *us*. As people.

Release! Now, if the bell goes 'ding-dong', and Matthew has a meeting in progress, then I know that I'm the one to answer.

And if it goes 'drrring' and Matthew is in, I know I can ignore it. (Or, if I'm in the bath, I know not to go shouting jokes downstairs – at least, not with the door open.)

We've found one drawback so far.

It's not often, is it, that a florist comes with a huge bouquet of flowers just for you? And if he does, part of the joy is seeing the red van and having a handsome man pass *you* the arrangement. Don't you think so?

Well, guess what happened only this week. The dozy florist rang the vicar's doorbell, even though the flowers were addressed to the lady of the house! I missed half the pleasure.

Still, Matthew was pleased to receive them on my behalf. And I suppose my old man deserves a bit of a treat. He's not often thanked for his labours.

12 Mothering Sunday

25th March

Happy Mothering Sunday! And if you have children, I hope they don't let you down quite so much as mine did a week ago. In church.

It was a family service which meant that, in place of Sunday School, we had a children's talk. My friend Rachel went up to the front and began by asking the children questions. I am convinced that that can be very dangerous for parents at the best of times. Last week proved disastrous as far as I was concerned.

Rachel's first question was, 'What makes you feel hurt?'

Hands shot up to give answers, with every gory answer offered, from bleeding knees to getting your head bashed in, to being sick. The boy making this latter suggestion was pretty graphic in his descriptions; Rachel had to thank him swiftly before we got any visual demonstrations.

It reminded me of a notice I once saw in a church magazine. It read:

WOULD THE CONGREGATION PLEASE NOTE THAT THE BOWL AT THE BACK OF CHURCH LABELLED 'FOR THE SICK' IS FOR MONETARY DONATIONS ONLY.

Last Sunday, Rachel tried to steer away from blood and gore. 'What *other* sorts of hurts have you experienced?' she asked.

And my children were the first to suggest answers.

'When your mum or dad smacks you,' said Philippa.

I didn't know whether to look totally innocent, ignore her, or glower at her. But I didn't think any of those ideas would ever have worked – people in our church know me far too well – so instead I smiled sweetly and congratulated her for being a brave girl to answer a question in church.

Inside I shrivelled up completely.

I might have recovered if, at that moment, Angus hadn't piped up.

'It hurts on the inside when your mum or dad just gets very cross with you,' he said. As he spoke he gave me a look: it was a mixture of a blush (because he's old enough to know that this was a risk which took him pretty near the bone) and a look of glee because he'd found an outlet to express a child's perspective on the unfairness of life.

I sank lower in my seat and wished to die.

Everyone else laughed. Not just a little chuckle. They fell about with gathering enthusiasm.

As the general mirth increased I plucked up the tiny bit of courage that was left and said, 'Well, at least you know we're a normal happy family.'

Some people, you see, think that we're models of perfection – or that we should be. They haven't twigged yet that vicars' families need God's forgiveness too.

Christine is one such person who used those very

words herself. I can still remember her face as I arrived in church on Mothering Sunday several years ago, when Philippa was still a baby. She looked into the pram and said admiringly, 'It must be great being the vicar's wife.'

I wasn't sure which aspect of being the vicar's wife she found so attractive.

'Well, your husband,' she said, 'he doesn't need to be reminded that Mothering Sunday should be special. I mean, the vicar gives flowers to everyone, doesn't he?'

What Christine said was true. What she didn't seem to realise was that in order for the vicar to achieve that, and for me to arrive in church with the baby looking spick and span, our home had been absolute mayhem earlier.

I bet she had pictures of Matthew bringing me breakfast in bed, with a special bunch of flowers for me, for being a mum. I bet she thought of me as some royal personage, being brought my baby: all clean, fed, dressed and ready to gurgle sweet smiles at me while I lazed there.

She can't have had any clue that I'd been up since half past six, not only shovelling mouthfuls of breakfast into the baby but also helping Matthew to put together bunches of flowers. Three daffodils, one twig of catkins, one piece of greenery, one spoonful of Weetabix... and I was trying to get Matthew to arrange the flowers prettily.

But I smiled sweetly at Christine. I do like pulling together with Matthew. And deep down I do know that my husband pulls together with me.

I'll just have to stop aiming at the impossible: teaching a man how to put together bunches of flowers. Artistically.

13 April Fool

1st April

This morning it's not the vicar's wife. April Fool! Today
it's the turn of the Husband Of The Vicar's Wife.

I reckon it's time for me to have a word. Everyone is
getting so sympathetic with the life that the vicar's *wife*
leads. Has anyone thought what life's like for her husband?

A clergy colleague of mine sidled up to me recently.
He spoke in a very confidential sort of voice. 'I do think
that it could be really hard for you ever to get another
decent job as vicar; your wife has been saying so much
on the radio.'

His remark reminded me of the time when I
preached at a church in Chester. At the start of the service, when I was being introduced to the congregation,
I was not welcomed with the usual spiel about my
church and work. Hoh-hoh no.

The vicar began, 'We welcome this morning Matthew
Grayshon as preacher.' He then paused, as if he were
still weighing up in his mind how to phrase his

sentiment. With a hint of a smile he said, 'Actually, Matthew is probably best known through his wife.'

There was a titter of laughter among the congregation. He then looked across to me, checking my reaction. 'In fact, you could describe Matthew as the Dennis Thatcher of the North.'

There was so much laughter I couldn't work out whether that was a compliment or sympathy.

So, a few weeks ago, just as my wife had finished spouting for the third time on this programme, the telephone rang. I picked it up and answered, 'Hello, Jane Grayshon's husband.'

Fortunately for me, the person at the other end had been listening to his radio.

But for all that Jane says in her confessions – and yes, I'm afraid they're all true – she doesn't tell you what life's like for me.

For example, when I'm not wearing my collar people ask me what I do, more for something to say than out of any real interest. I'm thinking of people like hairdressers who feel they must make conversation. When I tell them I'm a vicar, they seem to get an awful shock. I might as well be saying, 'I'm an ogre!' So I've taken to letting people in more gently.

Last week it was an insurance salesman whom I met at a friend's house. While we were being introduced I learned that he had just been promoted in his work for an insurance company.

'Aha,' I said, shaking his hand. 'You're into success and security? I'm into failure and frailty.'

He asked where I work.

'Most of my work is in visiting people's homes,' I said.

'Which company do *you* work for?' he asked casually. He was assuming that we were all in the same business as each other.

I had to think very fast. 'The glorious company,' I said.

'Oh yes?' There was the hint of question in his voice.

'Yes. The glorious company of the heavenly host.'

Clearly he did not understand me – despite the knowing nod he eventually gave.

'Oh aye. Are they a subsidiary of Allied Life then?'

I suppose you could say that. Except that the life which God gives is rather more abundant than the terminal bonus on any life assurance policy.

Other people start going peculiarly coy the minute they hear what I do. I find the school playground the most difficult, whenever I go to collect the children. Everyone keeps at such a safe distance, even pretending that I'm not there at all, that any onlooker would honestly think that I have a huge opaque bubble all around me making me invisible.

Or if people *have* to talk to me, they start trying to sound terribly religious. They will give torrents of excuses as to why they don't come to church. They will say, 'Of course, I don't go to your church because I live over in Cheshire. I go over the road to St Sainsbury's.'

'Oh yes,' I reply. 'Isn't that where Dick Fence is vicar?'

And then they blush. They go all stuttery. Because they have no idea whether the vicar of St Sainsbury's is Dick Fence or Jo Bloggs. They never go, do they? And then they wish they hadn't pretended to be religious; and so do I.

There's just one last thing. For all that Jane said about badges at the conference three weeks ago, she didn't tell you everything. She didn't tell you, for example, that someone looked at *her* name, Jane Grayshon, and asked if that was her real name or just a pen name.

I raised myself to my full height. 'It's her real name,' I replied. 'And *I* gave it to her.'

14   Body Beautiful

8th April

Yippeee! I'm really pleased with myself. On Friday I swam thirty-six lengths, which is half a mile. That means I've reached the target I set myself a couple of months ago, aiming to do a bit more each week until here I am now having got where I wanted. Don't you think half a mile is brill?

Anyone who knows me will tell you that such ecstacy about my achievements is fairly typical of me. In fact, at a church meeting in our home on Wednesday, the ten or so of us in the group were doing one of those self-awareness exercises. We split into pairs and each person had to think of one word to describe the other. To help us, we were given a list of words to choose from.

Having seen that one of the words on this list was 'Body Beautiful', I sat with a big grin, waiting for my partner, Tom, to choose his word. I was convinced that I knew what he would say.

Suddenly, after much studying of the list, Tom spoke.

'Competitive!' he said. 'That's the word for you, Jane.'

Huh!

I wished I had been sitting next to Albert across the room. He would definitely have chosen 'Body Beautiful'. But 'Competitive'?

Unfortunately, despite my worthy efforts to maintain a supply of excuses for myself, my pride began to deflate. My mind went straight to someone I know who is so competitive, his life consists of climbing social and professional ladders. And if the rungs are comprised of people, that's fine by him; *clonk*! He steps on them in order to get himself higher.

The thought that Tom might be accusing me of being like this filled me with horror.

Tom saw my face. 'Being competitive doesn't have to be bad,' he added kindly.

Oh no? Any attempts he might make to reassure me now seemed too late. I did not hear any of the meeting thereafter. By the end of the evening my spirits had flagged almost completely. I was torn between my excuses for myself and my desire to change into someone much nicer than I am. I tried to take myself in hand. I would see if the Bible would help. Turning to a familiar passage I read about the runner 'pressing on towards his goal'. There, take comfort from that, I told myself. The Bible says it's good to compete!

But then I read the competitor's goal: 'To know Christ, and the power of his resurrection.'

Gulp! That didn't help me at all. I'm not competitive enough concerning that!

Disgusted at myself, I gave up.

Happily for me, I was easily distracted. The very next morning we heard that my brother Pete and his wife had had a baby. I leapt into the car and zoomed to the hospital to visit them. Aaah, he was lovely. Only a few hours old, and there the baby lay in Pete's arms, looking up at him with intent gaze. Already I could see how that tiny little person was getting to know his dad.

And then the penny dropped. Of course: God is our Father! The competition to get to know him is simply a case of looking towards him, just like a baby to his dad!

I wouldn't mind being competitive towards that. Maybe I could forgive Tom for his nasty choice of word after all?

As for my swimming, I will say one thing. If you go to Runcorn swimming pool, and you want to know which of the early morning swimmers is me ... you'll know now, won't you?

I'm the one that's Body Beautiful.

15   Bottoms out for Perfect Skiing

15th April

We spent a few days' holiday after Easter up in bonny
Scotland. Thirteen of us took over two cottages in Glen-
coe. The scenery was majestic and the company great
fun. We had hoped we might have a bash at skiing but,
in the absence of snow, we had to content ourselves with
stories of skiing.

One of the thirteen, a schoolmaster, assured us that
his tale was absolutely true. I've discovered that people
tend to be extra truthful when they're talking to a vicar
(I hope they're as honest with God), so I must believe
what he told us one evening.

His school had arranged a skiing trip to Austria. One
member of staff took his wife, who had never skied
before. On the first morning she learned an elementary
rule of skiing: never have too many cups of coffee
before leaving your hotel. Halfway through the morning – with still two hours to go – she simply had to pluck
up courage to have a quiet word with her instructor.

'There's no loo here,' he said bleakly.

'But I *must* go!' she insisted.

The instructor realised her desperation. 'OK,' he agreed. 'D'you see those fir trees over there?' He pointed a little way off. 'You go there while I keep the group occupied over here.'

So off she went. At this point she rather cursed all the layers of clothing which have to be worn in order to keep warm, but she dug her sticks into the ground and hung her anorak over them. She undid the buckles of her ski dungarees, slipped them down and with sweet pleasure bent down to relieve herself.

Now, I don't know if you've ever done any skiing but, even if you haven't, you must have seen pictures of the professionals. So you'll know the position one is supposed to adopt: feet slightly apart, knees bent, leaning forward a little with bottom out ...

Of course, that is exactly the position this lady adopted in answer to the call of nature. The moment she bent her knees, she sensed a slight movement in her skis. She quickly tried to stand up but unfortunately her centre of gravity was all wrong – or rather, it was all correct for a good skier. As her skis began to slide forwards she grabbed for her poles. Too late! She merely gathered momentum and went sliding – beautifully – down the hill.

'Bottom out' was more than a little literal.

She was absolutely mortified. At the foot of the slope she made straight for her hotel room, totally unable to face anybody.

After a couple of days her husband, understanding though he was, became a little impatient with her hibernation. 'Look,' he said, 'I know how thoroughly embarrassed you've been, but we haven't paid good money for you to hide in this room all holiday. At least come to the bar with me tonight.'

She knew she had to overcome her timidity so she

agreed to go to a different hotel bar. There they met a man whose arm was bandaged. She thought it would be safe to express her sympathy with him.

He was very warm and friendly, and his eyes twinkled as he spoke.

'Thanks, but I must tell you how I fell. I couldn't take my eyes off this vision. You'll never believe this. There was this woman...'

Her mind swam at the prospect of listening to his tale without one flicker of recognition. Never had she experienced such humiliation.

Of course, one person who knows all about humiliation is a man who hung naked on the cross; for you and for me.

16 | The Wind Bloweth Where It Wilt in Hospital

In mid-April an ongoing illness took a very serious twist and I was suddenly rushed into hospital where I had to undergo an emergency operation. However, I felt enthusiastic to continue my broadcasts as soon as possible so, thanks to the producer driving miles with his tape recorder, I resumed this series within days of being discharged.

13th May

I am sorry to have missed you for the last three weeks while I've been in the tender care of Whiston Hospital. But don't feel too sorry for me because, despite the pretty grim reality of my illness, there have at least been moments which ensured that all was not sadness and woe.

One such moment repeated itself every time the doctors did a round of the ward examining their patients. Every day after my operation it was the same subject which dominated their minds. Whereas most people in our society introduce themselves with a gentle question such as, 'How are you?' these doctors would stick to their one track.

'Have you passed wind?' they would ask loudly, leaning forward with serious concern.

The first time, I wanted to reply that that is *not* how to speak to a vicar's wife.

By the end of two-and-a-half weeks I wanted to say, 'For goodness' sake – have *you* passed wind?'

A patient in hospital is supposed to console himself with the old saying: 'There's always someone worse off.' I discovered during this fortnight that that's not just a saying. It's really true. The reason why I can be so sure is that I was in the bed right next to her. She was the worst case in the whole hospital (if not the whole region) and she had had the worst operation of anyone. She told me. Often.

There were consolations. For example, I was in the hospital where Marmaduke works – you remember, Marmaduke from church. It was nice to see him every day. Except that he's so wretchedly cool as a doctor. Do you know, one day he sat in the visitor's chair beside my bed and announced calmly, 'I couldn't find your pulse on the way into hospital.' (He and his wife Mabel had been giving me a lift in their car when suddenly I had collapsed.)

Finding his detachment difficult to accept I asked, 'Why are you so calm about that?'

He looked down his nose at me, giving himself the appearance of a maligned camel. 'You were still breathing from time to time.'

'Did you tell Mabel?'

'She was driving,' he said, as if this were an adequate answer. Then, seeing the question remain in my face, he explained, 'There was no point in causing her to crash the car and having all three of us dead on arrival at hospital.'

Charming.

Yet, despite such apparent callousness, I did feel

thoroughly cared for. I especially appreciated the time when the staff nurse stood watching my attempt to walk only hours after the operation. Emphasising each word she said admiringly, 'You are smashing!' I liked that. It makes such a difference when others appreciate the efforts we make in life.

And all your cards – thank you for them. I particularly enjoyed the one from Albert which was much more than the usual, 'Get well soon.' Albert wrote, 'How *dare* they scar Body Beautiful?'

My sentiment precisely. But don't worry, Albert. You won't get the chance to see my scar.

... Not like the inmates on the ward.

Patients are peculiar. They spend all day showing one another their wounds. Sympathy is dished out according to the size of your scar or the number of tubes you have.

I had tubes here, there – yes, and everywhere, thank you. But it was my abdominal wound that won me the most points.

However much I wanted to guard my privacy, I'm afraid I didn't succeed. I got cornered by two patients simultaneously. They were admiring their wounds and I tried so hard to stay out of such a crude activity. I thought to myself, somebody like Marmaduke would manage to get out of this situation – he'd make some caustic remark! But I couldn't think of one quickly enough, and in the end I succumbed to let them have a peep.

Now, I've been called lots of things in my life. Only a few days earlier a doctor in X-ray had described me as 'a hosepipe with a kink in it'. But I've never heard anyone describe me in quite the same way as the patient looking at my wound.

'Oooh,' she said with awe. 'You look just like a Cornish pasty.'

It's a good job I know God loves me.

17   Devilled Kidneys and Bedpans

20th May

There was a nostalgic aspect of being back in hospital: nostalgia for the good old days when I was a nurse. In particular, the bedpans served to remind me about one of the practical jokes I used to get up to when I was on night duty.

You see, night duty can be so jolly tedious. The first night is always the worst: you're not in any rhythm of staying awake to mop fevered brows. Your whole body is screaming to kip down like the patients. You would even get into bed beside them at times. (Well, some of them.)

There was one night while I was a student that a friend and I decided we would have to do something to keep ourselves awake.

I ought to explain that on the ward where we were working, there was a newly qualified doctor who was absolutely dreadful. I assure you, I am not exaggerating. Some people have it and some people just don't. And she, poor soul, definitely didn't.

During the afternoon before our first night on duty in the medical ward, my friend and I moseyed along to the butcher's shop where we bought one animal kidney.

At around two o'clock in the morning, when we recognised the first signs that we were flagging, we unwrapped our parcel. Very carefully we placed the kidney into a bedpan, along with what you usually get in bedpans. Though I say it myself, it all looked pretty convincing.

Furthermore, there happened to be a patient in the ward who had been admitted that very day with a kidney complaint. So, just to add to the realistic touch, we labelled the bedpan with her name.

By the time the newly-qualified, unable-to-diagnose-anything doctor stuck her head round the door, we were well prepared for her. We did a round of the ward with her, as usual, giving her up-to-date information about each patient. We even plied her with a cup of tea to cheer her up. But before she left the ward we said casually, 'Oh, by the way, d'you think you could have a look at the contents of this bedpan? There's something a bit funny in there.'

She followed us into the sluice and then, seeing the vision we had so carefully prepared, she dived backwards away from it. I thought for a minute she might have a heart attack.

'Aaagh, it's a *kidney!*' she gasped, horrified.

We did our best to share her astonishment. 'Oh, doctor; it *can't* be,' we said.

'But it *is!*' she retorted with conviction. 'Look: there's its pelvis, there's the ureter, there's this...' She traced the shapes with her finger as she gave us her anatomy lesson. We didn't dare to look at each other; we would have cracked up with hilarity.

Then, proving her inability to distinguish human anatomy from an animal's, she said, 'It's a wee bit convoluted for a human kidney...' We held our breath while she considered for a moment. 'I suppose that must have been the pressure as it was being passed!'

She panicked, then. I still do not know how we kept our faces straight. I remember only the struggle to do so until, at last, she ran to the telephone to get the Professor out of his bed. At that point we had to put an end to her misery.

'Actually,' we grinned, 'it was a present, with love from our butcher.'

I do not know how long it took that doctor to get over that night. But it did make her take more care in future.

Unfortunately for me, I was not to emerge from such a prank unscathed. We were so elated by the success of our bedpan joke that we held on to the distant hope that we might find another gullible person to show our exhibit to.

I had not accounted for the morning visit of the hospital matron.

The rank of a matron is denoted by the height of her cap and, at six o'clock in the morning, just as we were beginning to waken our first patients, the matron whose frilled cap almost reached the ceiling entered. She was a woman with presence; a spinster who had risen to the top of the profession in this large Edinburgh teaching hospital.

'Nurrse!' That single word pierced through the curtains where I was washing a patient. 'Come with me!'

Meekly I followed her into the sister's office. I could sense her ire but was unable to guess how I deserved this exaggerated severity.

Her voice came low and terrifyingly steady. 'You did not summon me, Nurrse,' she growled.

Quaking, still unaware of my alleged fault, I said, 'I'm sorry, Matron, but I don't know what I should have summoned you for.'

Matron's lips tightened to a thin line. She was unaccustomed to any nurse – particularly a student – daring to answer back.

'The bedpan.' She pointed to the wall through which was the sluice. Immediately I felt myself flush with realisation and guilt.

'That, Nurrse, is a placenta.' Every word was taut and clipped. 'One of your patients has had a miscarriage!' Her voice was rising sharply. 'When did it happen, Nurrse?'

Panic swelled within me until I almost choked. Then, remembering an ancient Sunday School lesson when I had been threatened by an equally terrifying teacher as to the consequences of telling lies, I drew a deep breath.

'Actually, Matron,' I said quietly, mustering every grain of courage I had, 'that was a practical joke in the night, from our butcher.'

A long silence elapsed, during which Matron's face did not even twitch.

'Oh,' she spoke at last, straightening her hands in front of her apron and turning to leave. 'A very good one, Nurrse.'

My report from that matron was the best I ever had.

18   The Importance of Net Curtains

27th May

I have decided that I hate convalescing. For a start, people ask how you are but they don't listen to your answer. Have you ever noticed? Especially if you look well and suntanned, as I do after lazing in the sun so much in our garden this week.

I think what happens is that the question, 'How are you?' becomes so routine, it becomes a sort of chant. It goes from high notes to low: 'Hi, how are you?'

And the reply echoes the tune exactly; high to low: 'Fine thanks. How are you?'

I did an experiment. I discovered that you can change the words and people don't even notice.

'Hi, how are you?'

'Terrible thanks. How are you?'

As long as you keep the tune the same it doesn't matter what words you say. In fact one day I was really naughty and I used a swearword, still chanted with the same tune. No effect.

It made me wonder if people intone words to God in the same way, and then call it 'prayer'.

No wonder they don't hear God answer.

Another hateful aspect of this convalescing business is the swing from one good day to the next when you feel ghastly. Last week I got properly stumped.

Matthew had to go out, and we couldn't think how I could answer the door to the doctor when I was in agony upstairs in bed. I certainly couldn't trail all the way downstairs.

And then Matthew had a brainwave. Before he left he supplied me with a front door key so that, when the doctor came, I could throw the key out of the window for him to let himself in. What an excellent system! Well, *we* thought so.

The doctor was mortified.

'Huh huh,' he tried to chuckle as he stood beneath my window. I had no idea why he felt so awkward until he muttered, 'Bit like Romeo and Juliet, this...'

I wasn't well enough to give it another thought; it became apparent that he did not share my nonchalance. When he had finished his visit he became rather agitatedly self-conscious.

'I'm glad my car has a sticker explaining "Doctor Visiting", he said. 'And I think I shall carry my doctor's bag very obviously as I go out. After all, we don't want the neighbours talking if they watch the comings and goings at the vicarage.'

On Tuesday Marmaduke demonstrated the same awareness of the neighbours – though, predictably, his reaction was different. He had called round, not as a doctor, but because he had an appointment to speak to the vicar. At coffee time the two of them popped upstairs to keep me company and cheer my flagging spirits.

In the absence of chairs, Matthew sat on the edge of

the bed but Marmaduke leaned against the window. Then, just as he was about to go, he drained the last dregs of coffee from his cup and lifted the net curtain. With the driest tone he announced, 'I think everyone should get a chance to see there's a strange man in the bedroom with the vicar's wife!'

He turned and smiled in a self-satisfied way. 'That'll give them some gossip.'

I was very glad I knew that everyone was out. But I didn't tell Marmaduke.

19   Just a Minute

3rd June

I've been fantasising. It comes from being cooped up convalescing for too long, and listening to too much radio. Have you heard the Radio 4 programme, *Just A Minute*? Well, I've listened to so many episodes of it now that I feel ready to tackle Clement Freud and Peter Jones myself. I really fancy being alongside the professionals on the panel. Especially if they expect a vicar's wife to be all meek and mild and speechless: I'd enjoy giving them a shock. I guess I might not be too bad at that either.

Matthew says I'd be very good at interrupting the others. Huh! Still, it would be good to be awarded points for doing so. That would make a pleasant change.

I gather that the guest speaker is invariably given the chance to talk about something they know a lot about; something which they have experienced. So I reckon I could be given one of two subjects. If I'm lucky I'd be given 'Practical Jokes While You Were Nursing', and I could tell them about devilled kidneys. But I've no doubt that at some point they would drag up the subject of vicars' wives.

Well, that could be my big chance, couldn't it? I could tell them, then; I mean, really sock it to the world about what it's like being a vicar's wife. None of your idealised stories; I would give them the unadulterated truth.

For a start, I would say how glad I am that we don't have video telephones because, as you know, I conduct calls about baptisms and stuff in all sorts of bizarre circumstances. Only last week during the heatwave, as I lazed in the garden with only two things on – and one of those was my wedding ring – I was thinking how glad I was that I could answer the telephone without the other person seeing me. (Oops, I'd have to be careful not to repeat the word 'telephone' or I'd lose a mark.)

I could go on to tell them about my Confessions, though no doubt they wouldn't even have heard of BBC Radio Merseyside, seeing as most of them on that programme are chauvinistic Southerners. That might give me an advantage, though, because it might make the other panelists want to listen, and then they would be less likely to interrupt me. And then I might win!

Mind you, if I mentioned Radio Merseyside, I'd have to omit 'BBC' or they could have me up for repetition of 'B'.

Well if they did, and then my subject was passed over for one of them to talk about, I would soon get my revenge! I'd have my finger on the buzzer ready to be utterly ruthless. If they said anything about vicars' wives all running Mothers' Union meetings and wearing uniformly dowdy clothes, I'd say, 'Deviation! That's wrong!' Because I've never run a Mothers' Union meeting in my life. And, hopefully, I'd have made sure I was wearing my most outrageous clothes to prove that vicars' wives aren't all dowdy all the time.

And if they had the temerity to imply that a vicar's

wife is someone who cleans and cooks and makes cups of tea and cucumber sandwiches at the vicarage, while the vicar is the one who talks to people about God, then I would shout, 'Deviation again!' Because a vicar is just as capable of cleaning and cooking – isn't he? – and his wife is allowed to talk about God just as much as he is. If people want to talk about church, that's different, and much more boring – I *always* refer them to the vicar. But discussions about God – they're as much my business as they are yours, and I find them helpful, and stimulating, as I'm sure you do.

We can't leave the vicar to have all the fun.

20 The Parish Weekend

10th June

Our whole church spent all of last weekend away together. It was a good weekend with seventy-two of us together. So we saw more of each other than in our usual Sunday bests. We saw how people really are – like over breakfast (that speaks volumes).

On the first morning I had to tell Angus off for something, poor boy, and he glowered back at me. I said, 'Listen, Angus, you must learn to stop pulling sour faces. Let's make an agreement: if you do it again this weekend you'll pay a fine of 2p every time.'

Well, you-can-guess-who leaned across the breakfast table.

'Can I pay £1 in advance?' he whispered. His eyes sparkled with glee: he had been determined to loathe the whole weekend. It was too unclinical for him. 'It'd be worth £1 to be allowed to look as miserable as I feel.'

Unfortunately for his argument, Marmaduke's eyes spoke louder than his words. His dry asides provided one of the prime sources of amusement.

On the Saturday evening Albert stood up with several announcements. He said that he used to believe that only one good thing has ever come from Yorkshire to this side of the Pennines, and that was the vicar! (Matthew's last parish was in Yorkshire.) Everybody clapped and cheered Matthew – including myself – but I thought, Charming! So the vicar's wife is merely an appendage to the vicar, is she? She doesn't count as having any value of her own?

When the clapping had died down Albert said, 'But this weekend I've discovered that I was wrong. Two good things have come from Yorkshire...'

Great, I thought. I'm being appreciated at last.

'Because this weekend I've met Mick,' he continued.

Now Mick is a case and a half. He's a huge guy – over six feet tall with a big, huge, imposing don't-bother-fighting-me body. I'd sat behind him in the first meeting and I reckoned his neck must be about the same size as my waist. He's the sort of guy who makes Cyril Smith look anorexic.

Mind you, he is amazing. He had come to the weekend in order to tell his story. He told us how he used to drink twenty pints a night, no problem, and then fight for money. He had been a long-distance lorry driver until one day, quite out of the blue and against all his macho image, he found himself going into church. And while he was there, sitting at the back as inconspicuously as a man his size could, the curate – a small guy under five feet tall – felt he should go over to pray with Mick. He said to God, 'What, *me*, pray with *him*? No way!' But he did and do you know, while he did so Mick had to lie down he was so bowled over by the power of the Holy Spirit. And here is Mick today, a changed man who's given up his job in order to drive a bus around the miners' estates in Yorkshire, telling the Good News of Jesus.

So yes, I could cheer and clap for Mick. In fact it left me with a pretty big question for myself. Have I allowed God to do as much through me as he does through Mick? I had a nasty feeling that the truthful answer was no.

But then, on Monday morning, the telephone rang.

'Hello,' said the voice. 'I wanted to thank you for the weekend.'

'You want Matthew,' I replied. 'I'm awfully sorry, he's out.'

'No,' he said. 'I wanted you.'

'Me?' I asked him. 'But I can't claim to have done any of the work behind the scenes this year. Matthew did everything himself.'

'Jane,' he said, 'you reminded us that laughter and fun and being bubbly are a part of being alive. You showed that God isn't only about being serious. It meant a lot to laugh as you enabled us to. We wanted to thank you for that.'

And I thought, Oh. So maybe we *do* all have our own value, even if we feel a mere appendage. Maybe there are more than two good things which have come across from Yorkshire after all?

21   He Looks Like a Vicar!

17th June

'Jane, I don't know if you can understand how hard it is,' said Amanda, a friend of mine since school days, 'to think of the vicar, who looks so holy in church, as some-one who has been eating wobbly orange jelly only half an hour earlier!'

I checked myself from replying that eating orange jelly is the least of what Matthew can get up to only half an hour before church.

Amanda was trying to explain her strong reaction to seeing Matthew in a dog collar. Although we had kept in touch with one another by letter for years, this was the first time she had been to stay with us since university days.

On her arrival she had had an immediate taste of our lifestyle. In the middle of her first meal with us Matthew had looked at his watch and suddenly begun to stuff his last wobbly spoonfuls into his mouth.

'I must get myself changed and out if I'm going to be in time to sort everyone out at church,' he had spluttered quickly. 'The confirmation service starts in only an hour.' And he had fled upstairs.

It was only a few minutes later, when we were finishing our own helpings at a more leisurely speed, that Amanda had gone silent.

'Are you all right?' I asked, concerned.

'It's Matthew,' she said. I followed her gaze through into the kitchen where he was doing up his shoe laces. I saw nothing unusual about him.

She swallowed hard. 'He's – he's a *vicar!*'

'Don't be silly,' I snorted. 'You've known Matthew for twenty years. You know perfectly well he's a vicar.'

'Yes, but – I've never seen him – kind of – *look* like a vicar. I've always seen him as a person.'

'Makes a change,' I muttered, gathering the plates. 'Most people see only Matthew the vicar without realising that there's a real, pulsating person under there.'

Amanda did not hear me. She continued to stare at the vision.

I began to feel frustrated. 'How can you forget that Matthew's a vicar when you see a sign at the front door as you arrive, saying in capital letters, "VICARAGE"?'

She replied that a sign outside doesn't help her when our house inside doesn't look like a real vicarage.

'So what does a "real" vicarage look like?' I asked. Intrigue began to replace my former frustration.

Amanda's description was vivid. Coffee out of a chipped cup; cold, bland paintwork on the walls; a downstairs cloakroom-cum-loo smelling of institutional disinfectant, probably with a slab of old and dirty, cracked soap at the basin; a shabby-looking piano for bashing out hymns rather than being part of an aesthetic art form; and, of course, the vicar's wife would be wearing Oxfam clothes.

It was all a neat caricature. Amanda's description caused me to wonder how many people put vicars into such a box, neatly labelled (no doubt): 'Pious nit-wits.' I squirmed at the very idea. Perhaps, I realised, that is why Matthew and I take extra trouble to let our home express something of our personalities. We both loathe being labelled.

However, there was one occasion when Matthew thoroughly enjoyed turning the tables. For once *he* labelled someone else: it was the undertaker. As he stood chatting with her at the supermarket check-out he took great glee in saying aloud what her job is.

It's not the undertaker herself for whom I feel most sorry. It's the till-lady. There she was, perfectly happy serving two ordinary customers (as she thought), when Matthew announced both their jobs. Her mouth dropped open like a fish.

'Oh God!' she said, rather more appropriately than she realised.

With a reaction which was a cross between amusement and total panic, she called across to her mate on the next till. 'An undertaker and a vicar at my till... at the same time!' They giggled, but only to cover their embarrassment. It was quite clear that her idea of vicars and undertakers did not include them doing anything so human as shopping.

Thank God he doesn't box us like that. In fact the resurrection we celebrated at Easter time is all about him lifting us out of boxes.

22 Away from It All?

24th June

We've had a few days of peace. We needed to get right away from it all, so we disappeared to a beautifully quiet little cottage at the end of a dirt track. It was real back-to-nature stuff: there wasn't even any electricity.

... Which did actually present problems with my hair-dryer on the day I needed to look clean and lovely. Because, guess what. Our away-from-it-all-ness was totally ruined when a crew from the BBC came to film us. They had persuaded us that our secluded lakeside setting would make a picturesque backdrop for my part in a new series: which may have been true, but if you watch it you'd better admire my hair.

It wasn't bad actually; they were so nice. In fact, if I'm really honest, by the time I was doing the serious talk bit, I felt as if I were chatting with a few friends instead of millions of people. It was all terribly relaxed.

All except for a swan who vied for the star role. While

I sat at the lakeside spouting philosophically, from the corner of my eye I saw something white glide into view on the lake.

'Concentrate, Jane!' I told myself. 'You're supposed to be talking about healing, not wondering what this swan's doing.' But as it reached the water's edge, it began to walk to within a few paces of us, with its flippers squelching loudly as they slapped the shore – shooooch! And then it stretched up to full height and opened its wings to display a huge span until, in mid-sentence, I collapsed.

'I can't talk seriously with that thing there!' But I had no need to apologise: everyone gave way to their pent-up laughter, apparently having been eyeing it with terror. The producer decreed that the second it hissed, we should run for our lives.

Most of our holiday, though, was undisturbed. On only one of our long walks did we meet someone. We had made the mistake of following a footpath which drew close to a golf course and a golfer was searching in the undergrowth.

'I say,' he called out in a distinctly superior Oxford accent. 'How much d'you charge for finding a lost ball?'

I surveyed the nettles between us. '£50!'

'£50?' he repeated with shocked incredulity. 'That's a bit steep, isn't it?'

'Yes,' I agreed. 'But when you work for the BBC you have to get your money from somewhere.'

Suddenly, his whole manner towards me changed. He began to speak as if I were someone to respect instead of the schoolkid he had been patronising.

'Oh...' it was an awed sound, just like when people hear that Matthew is a vicar. 'You work for the BBC?'

I nodded. I didn't explain that it would be more accurate to say that I 'volunteer' for the BBC; just as I 'volunteer' to do the work of a vicar's wife; just as I 'volunteer' to do a woman's work. No, I was on holiday from such campaigns.

And now we're back, straight in at the deep end. You may have heard that Chester Diocese is celebrating its 450th birthday next Sunday by having a huge day-long celebration at the racecourse. Since my husband is one of five organisers I hope you can imagine how hot our phone is at present.

I may see you there next week... though how shall you know I'm me?

23   VIPs and How to Become One

1st July

'When you don't know a vicar,' said Anne on Thursday morning, as she packed my children into her car to give them a lift, 'I know you won't like me saying this Jane, but most of us do think of them as only working on Sundays.'

Matthew had been delayed at the Roo Dee (the race-course) preparing for today's celebrations, leaving me car-less. He had been there since six o'clock in the morning, marking out precise positions for the Biggest Top in Europe.

'You just don't have any idea of the sorts of things they get up to,' she said.

I must say that this week has brought an extra dimension into Matthew's life. And mine. I've been intrigued to hear his mutterings as he's flopped into bed and gone over odd things in his mind... some odder than others.

'Thank heavens I've managed to avoid five mobile loos landing up in the middle of the Big Top.' Or, 'I must make sure the hot food man stays *down*-wind of the canvas cathedral. We can't have the smell of fried onions wafting into the communion service like incense.'

His mind has been on one marquee in particular. They've had such problems over what to call it.

It began as the 'VIP Tent'. But that was ludicrous. As Matthew said, you can't have Christians deliberately disregarding the fact that every individual is a VIP. Rank and position have nothing whatever to do with being important to God, even if you are an MP or a Lord Lieutenant or an Archbishop.

So then it became the 'Special Guests' Tent'. But that had to go because of people like me. (I pointed out, you see, that I was sure I could talk my way into a Special Guests' Tent. After all, I'm ME! And of course, dahling, I'm the vicar's wife...and not just any old vicar's wife, but MATTHEW's wife. Isn't that special?)

After the next committee meeting the name was changed, yet again, to 'Invited Guests' Tent'. Huh.

But late on Friday afternoon I heard that I might get into it yet. I'm to interview the Archbishop. There must surely be possibilities of my engineering something there?

'Aren't you terrified?' asked Anne again.

'No, why?' I asked in reply. 'He should be terrified of me! And if he's not, he doesn't know me very well!'

Of course I might persuade someone that I need to do the interview in the Archbishop's car on his way through Chester. I've always fancied being chauffeur-driven with a police escort.

I'm looking forward to this whole day. I've given Matthew a badge saying, '...And I'm her husband.' But I have told him that while he wears it he must be very careful whom he's standing next to.

One anxiety I do have is that I can't stay on my feet all day. I shared my worry with a young vicar who recently had to retire due to ill health.

'How are you going to cope when you need a rest?' I asked him.

He told me that his wife is running a tent where there are several screens and, when he feels too weary, he'll slip behind one of them to sit quietly. Why didn't I do likewise?

I thanked him. 'But really I need to lie down,' I said.

'We could always lie on the grass,' he offered.

For a moment I could picture the two of us – one vicar and another vicar's wife – lying in the grass; and I could only hope that nobody would pop their head behind the screen and get the wrong impression.

24   The Queen's Arms

8th July

Mmmmm, there's nothing quite so delicious as a little bite of something when you know you shouldn't really be there.

You'll probably have gathered, I made it! I'm referring to the special marquee last Sunday, where I had been made welcome not just for a cuppa, but also for home-made scones piled high with fresh cream and strawberry jam.

I had two worries. First, my beloved was too busy to join me and he wasn't even invited in (aaah). Secondly, the Archbishop was much more chatty, pulling my leg, saying I looked like a vulture, than when I had had the microphone switched on to interview him.

His arrival shortly beforehand had brought to light some interesting remarks. Among the flurry of camera activity when the VIP car drew up, I could hear a muttered, 'Oh damn. He *said* he'd put a new film in for me but he's been too busy doing other things...' I smiled. Typical vicar's wife!

And then there was the slightly sour, if smiled whisper, 'Trust so-and-so to get a special introduction.'

Why am I telling you this? Because it illustrates the fact that we're all human. Vicars and their wives don't belong among the angels; they're the same as you, maybe worse. We all get frustrated, irritated, cross. Why don't we help one another? God can forgive us – so long as we don't hide in shame from him.

In fact the day went exceptionally well. The frayed tempers were few and far between, having far less consequence than the fact that so much was so good. Seventeen thousand people altogether gathered in the huge canvas cathedral, spreading outside to fill the racecourse. People have described how they were walking round the walls of the city when they heard the swell of so many people singing rise gently to greet them. And the team spirit between all those organising and enjoying the day was quite remarkable.

It was fun, if enlightening, to meet people from all over the diocese, some of whom we hadn't seen for years. One such person was Keith.

'D'you know, Jane,' he said, 'more than once we've been driving near Runcorn and we have attempted to pop in and see you. But it's such a confusing new town, we always get lost.'

Keith was not the type of person who lacks initiative.

'Couldn't you have asked where we were?'

'Oh, I did that,' he replied. 'I stopped by a pub where a group of lads were hanging around. I asked for directions to the vicarage but they looked totally blank. One of them must have thought the vicarage was the name of a pub, because he replied that he only knew the way to the Queen's Arms.'

As a matter of fact, I reckon that the Queen's Arms is a fairly accurate description of our vicarage.

Finally, at the end of the afternoon, a man came up to

me, obviously bursting to share an important observation.

'You know your confessions of a vicar's wife series?' he asked. He looked as if he was about to make his confession to me. 'Well, I must tell you...'

He leaned closer to my ear.

'We're having a quiz at our church social on Saturday.' He gave a knowing wink. 'One of the questions I'm proposing for the media section is, "Who is known as Body Beautiful?"'

I wished I had put on a more stunning dress.

25   Sunday Lunch

15th July

We do enjoy Sunday lunch. I try to cook a bit of a treat on a Sunday, like roast meat. And I'm not sure if we're very different from most families, but I aim for it to be ready at about one o'clock.

It is almost guaranteed that at one o'clock every Sunday the vicarage telephone will ring. If it were for something really urgent, that would be one thing, but so far, in the ten years since my old man has been a vicar, it has only ever been for little queries which could easily have waited.

Is it because everyone knows that the vicar is likely to be in at lunchtime? Or are lots of people like the chap who actually told Matthew that he had needed a few cans on his Sunday booze-up in order to pluck up courage to speak to a vicar?

I have no idea. What I do know is that I've almost got to the point of swearing. (Oops, you're not supposed to know that.)

I bet you'll write to tell me about a vicar's wife whom

you know, who is *always* gracious and pleasant and loving and kind, at all times. Well, I'm very pleased for you, but I'm afraid I'm not so nice as that. I get very frustrated.

Last Sunday was one such occasion. Exactly on the dot of one o'clock: dring dring.

Grrrr, I thought. I had just got the children sitting at the table, where they were reluctantly carrying out instructions to be polite to our visitor. Matthew was at the church hall having a special lunch with the Mayor to celebrate some Boys' Brigade awards.

At the sound of the telephone I scowled, leaving my gravy to go lumpy. As I walked across the kitchen I even rehearsed possible nasty things I could say when I picked up the receiver, like, 'Hello, lunchtime!' or, 'Hello, and I'm sorry the vicar's out.'

I cannot tell you how glad I am that I did not do that. I would never have forgiven myself. This time, it was not something which could have waited. It was a lady phoning for her husband who had had a heart attack and was in a state. He wanted the vicar to come quickly.

That jerked me out of any indulgent thoughts about a relaxed Sunday lunch. Suddenly I was flying around trying to beg, borrow or even steal a car so I could go and find Matthew. Once at the church hall I had to disturb the Mayor's ceremony, drag the vicar out and shoo him off immediately to the man in distress.

And equally suddenly I realised afresh that it's a privilege – yes, a privilege – to be disturbed. Because, for some people like this man, a phone call to the vicarage is the only step they will ever take in all their lives to make contact with God.

I came home to find my children still sitting on their best behaviour, making admirable endeavours to keep the visitor entertained, but wondering why on earth Mummy had said, 'It's lunchtime.'

Worse misunderstandings followed. When I heard of the rumours, I didn't know whether to laugh or cry; I never do. There were those who wondered if the vicar had skived out of the Mayor's ceremony, because he preferred going out with his wife.

Meanwhile, the lady who had phoned was disappointed that this vicar took forty minutes to arrive.

But being misunderstood is all part of the job. It shouldn't put us off.

But – er – just one thing. If you're phoning your vicar, *do* ask yourself if you have to do so at a mealtime. One day you just might get your head bitten off – even by the nicest vicar's wife in the world!

26

Cutting Everyone – and every-thing – down to size

22nd July

There's one thing I must say about the folk in our parish. They don't half keep one – well, me – down to size.

After my impassioned plea last week for no one o'clock phone calls, Albert came up to me on Monday with a wink.

'We were *all* going to phone you at lunchtime yesterday,' he assured me, 'but you'd gone out for lunch.'

I wouldn't put it past them, either, to lodge their protest at what I say about them on radio.

Do you know, one man who is always game for a laugh recounted to Matthew and myself what he and four friends once did to another vicar. Perhaps he told us in order to warn us that we had better watch how we behave.

This particular vicar was – how can I put it? – he was not known for his patience. So late one evening, feeling it was time to teach their vicar a lesson, the five friends decided they would each telephone him in turn.

The first one said, 'Hello, is Eric there please?'

The vicar didn't know anyone by that name.

Ten minutes later the second one asked the same, and then the third. By the time the fourth one asked for Eric, the priest replied with pretty juicy words.

And then the fifth one phoned. *He* said, 'Hello, Eric here. I'm just calling to ask if there are any messages for me.'

That poor vicar! I wonder if the episode did help him to grow in patience. I'm glad that when God decides to teach us a lesson, he doesn't use such mean tricks.

At least, I don't think he does. However, I am beginning to think that a sense of humour is a God-given part of our survival. It percolates through even serious and holy institutions. I only pray that God can see the funny side, too.

I must not say exactly where this story took place, but it was at a Catholic seminary which takes itself very seriously indeed. Perhaps that was part of the trouble.

It was announced that communion would be administered slightly differently for once, and according to the Church of Scotland tradition. The loaf was to be passed round the chapel and each student was to take his own portion of bread.

The idea for collusion arose during an incident the previous week, when too much wine had been poured out, and the college principal had become increasingly anxious not to have to drink all the remnants alone. Thus every time he had proferred the cup, he had urged each communicant in as holy a voice as he could, 'Draw deeply.'

Someone, somewhere, derived from that a mischievous idea. The suggestion was whispered between every student that, when the loaf was passed round, each man should take only a tiny crumb.

And that is what they did. Thus, when they had finished, more than three-quarters of the loaf was returned to the principal. Apparently his face was a picture as he gazed at the plate, still laden, for he was the one who had to consume all that remained!

He had his revenge, however. He made the students sing lengthy and dirge-like hymns while he solemnly ate. It took him so long that the morning service was late in finishing and they all missed their breakfast.

The only stomach not rumbling throughout the lectures that morning was the principal's. No one had noticed the twinkle in his eye while the singing had gone on, and on, and on....

27 Good-for-the-Bowels Macaroni

29th July

I feel quite weary of trying to keep my children quiet in church. I am even beginning to wonder whether it is always right to try. Should children always pay for adults' pleasure?

I'm expected to be the model of perfection in all things at church, and so are my offspring. Nobody seems to twig that the vicar's wife is one person in the congregation whose husband is never there to help. I have every sympathy with other parents who come on their own; for example, when their other half refuses to come anywhere near church.

I learned at a wedding this summer that, however hard I try, I can't seem to win. Let me explain.

I found myself looking after not only my two children, but also four toddler-sized bridesmaids and page boys whose bright faces lined the front pew. I was not entirely on my own: two parents had been placed next to the little cherubs at the other end of the pew. Nevertheless, I feared that entertainment might be

rather uphill work, so I had prepared ways to keep them quiet (the children, that is).

I rather went to town. I had a Mary Poppins bag full of surprises, with four of each activity. Most of the sermon was spent with me judging when it was time to bring out the next distraction.

I started them off with some little books with bright pictures. Those didn't last long. The children sensed that they were being kept quiet and they decided to have more fun than that. Very soon they had set up a competition to see who could make the loudest noise: the one bashing the spine of his book against the ledge in front, or the one dropping them on the floor.

I quickly recognised that it was time for a change; to do something more active. I passed along four identical tiny bags, each containing a length of wool and some pieces of raw macaroni. Knowing that the parents at the other end may have been called upon to help, I had labelled the bag, 'For threading and making necklaces.' Past experience had convinced me that this was a great way to keep children quiet in church.

In tiny writing I had added, 'Pure wholemeal macaroni. Good for the bowels.' (The nurse in me will out, you know.)

Unfortunately the parents got the giggles. I felt faintly responsible for creating further distractions.

Three out of the four children became thoroughly absorbed and very content. But I could not have anticipated that the fourth little girl would try eating the stuff. Raw macaroni! And what bothered me more than the effect it might have on her stomach was the fact that it crunched. Loudly. Right in the middle of the sermon.

I couldn't stop her. Nobody could, though several people became involved in trying. In true Joyce Grenfell style I leaned along, smiling sweetly to her and pointing as pleasantly but firmly as I could to indicate the wool for threading. But I made no difference whatsoever. In fact it is possible that I made things worse, because she smiled back to me, and while she was smiling her mouth was open and her teeth were more evident; so every crunch seemed to resound with a crack which echoed around the church, unmuffled by her lips.

That bridesmaid crunched her way through a whole necklace length of raw wholemeal macaroni.

Soon the others proudly finished their necklaces and put them on. *They* then wanted something to eat, too. One kind granny leaned forward with chocolate buttons which gave me horrifying visions of sticky chocolate paw-marks all over their beautiful bridesmaid's dresses. I managed to accept them gratefully for myself and I pulled out some raisins for the little ones, all carefully measured out in four of those little containers you buy films in.

All told, I thought I had done very well... though there was one problem with such creative entertainment. As the organ started for the final hymn, the little bridesmaids and page boys joined the procession – and then I saw them with a different pair of eyes. Their beautiful satin outfits were still adorned with clumsy necklaces made of wholemeal, good-for-the-bowels macaroni.

Only the cruncher looked good in the photographs.

28 The Man You Now Have Is Not Your Husband

5th August

It's amazing how many people come up to me during the week with their anecdotes concerning what I've said on this programme. Since my mention of a wedding last week, I have been regaled with several tales of weddings and wedding mishaps.

One vicar told me advisedly, 'I give special attention to the choice of hymns.'

His precise manner of talking gave the impression that any rules of etiquette were of paramount importance to him.

'For example,' he explained with a hint of a smile, 'one must steer the couple away from singing, "Be present, awful Father, to give away this bride."'

I could feel an urge to tell him that that was the most harmless of wedding hymns, but I knew I must desist. He was such a gentleman, it would have been an intrusion into the politeness between us if I had quoted the old Wesley hymn, 'With thee all night I mean to stay / And wrestle till the break of day.'

'And,' he went on with a sparkling grin, 'if the wedding is, um, rushed, and especially if the bride is obviously, um, expecting, I do point out the pitfalls of that favourite hymn, 'Love divine'.'

'Pitfalls?' I asked him.

'Mmmm.' His eyes twinkled in a conspiratorial way. 'Verse 3. "Finish then Thy new creation"!' He fumbled in his pocket for his pure white handkerchief, and laughed into its folds with innocent glee.

At least *that* vicar was alert to the words. Not like another whom I know (not Matthew this time!). I think his excuse was that he had done two weddings already on one particular Saturday, but without a doubt he was running on auto-pilot.

He asked the bride to repeat her vows:

'I Susan...'

'I Susan...'

'Take you, Brian...'

'Take you, Brian...'

'To be my wedded wife...'

'To be my wedded ... I'm not saying *that*!' she exclaimed.

The vicar was jerked from his dreaminess. 'Oh no. We mean, to be my wedded *husband*.'

And he paused for a moment before starting again. They even rewound the tape recording the service, so that it would sound as if history had been perfect.

However, there could be no rewinding of tapes when a rather pompous man named Dennis was to read the Bible passage at a wedding where he was best man. Now, Dennis liked to think he was good at everything, so although he was unfamiliar with churches, he would never have admitted such a thing. He was at pains to point out that he certainly did not need to be shown his way around a Bible, 'a schoolboy book', as his attitude indicated. In fact, he was pretty scornful at having to endure a rehearsal for the wedding at all.

The text which Dennis had been asked to read was written down for him: 1 John chapter 4. The couple wanted this passage about God's love, beginning at verse 18, 'Perfect love casts out all fear...'

Good old Dennis didn't know that 1 John 4:18 refers to John's first letter, and that that is different from John's Gospel. So, when he mounted the lectern steps, he turned unwittingly to the Gospel. Verse 18 of chapter 4 reads: 'The fact is, you have had five husbands and the man you now have is not your husband.'

I'm glad they had a rehearsal.

29 Prescription for Disaster

12th August

My old man went away on Friday. It's the start of his
summer holiday and he's gone sailing round the west
coast of Scotland. No women or children allowed.

I wouldn't want you to feel too sorry for me being left
all alone. It's all right, because, you see, whenever he
goes on holiday it's always the same. He's always so tired
that for the first week of any holiday he's in a foul mood.
Well, this year I have been relieved of enduring that. He
can sail into the sunset and be as grumpy as he likes. I
won't even know about it.

And the best bit is that when he comes back, we're setting off immediately for our family holiday together. By
the time we go he'll be relaxed for a change. I'm really
looking forward to that.

In the meantime, I'm left for a week in the vicarage
without the vicar. Prescription for disaster! Even man-
ning the phone – or should I say, personing it – I could
put people off ever coming near a church. I had better
not do that. There are enough people in the world who

do that. Matthew has often said that a phone call to the vicar about a baptism, or a wedding, is the nearest some people ever dare go in coming towards God. So I mustn't discourage them.

No, I shall content myself in finding a few benefits from the man of the house being away. There must be some advantages; although the only one I can give so far is that I shan't have to find things for him all week.

It's interesting. On the radio recently I heard a panel of big-wigs sounding sickeningly knowledgeable about various topics. At one point they were discussing what they thought might be the best invention for the coming century. A professor suggested a computer which could help you find things that you'd mislaid: diary, specs, papers.... The only woman on the panel observed rather wryly that such a computer had been invented a long time ago, and it was called a wife.

Men can make themselves sound so miserable as they wander around the house helplessly saying, 'Where are my keys?' or, 'I can't find my socks.'

Just before he left on Friday, Matthew found a new way of asking for help. He stood by the bookshelf mumbling, 'We used to have an atlas.'

I resisted jumping to his aid. I simply answered that we still do.

'It used to be on this shelf,' he went on, still not addressing me directly, but giving the distinct impression that I was meant to hear him and help him.

'It *used* to be here,' he repeated, more strongly.

I did not succeed in resisting him for long. I got up, went over and picked up the atlas from right in front of his nose.

Why can't men simply admit that they're hopeless at searching for things? Or even ask directly for help, instead of using subtle hints?

I'd better be careful what I say, because actually I am

missing my old man very much. And the children are missing him too. They have been talking about him non-stop. In fact, listening to them this week I have learned a lot about how mine see the life of a vicar.

The best statement came from Philippa. She was in the back of the car chatting and squabbling with a number of other children and I suspect that on top of their boredom, a touch of rivalry was creeping into the relationship.

A boy, aged seven, whose father is a doctor, pulled out his trump card. In a loud, gloating voice he decreed, 'Anyway, *my* daddy sees dead bodies.'

There was just a hint of hesitation before Philippa gave her reply.

'So what?' she said with a distinct air of superiority. '*My* daddy digs them into the ground!'

30

Panic Meets Composure
(or, Working for the Vicar?)

19th August

I've had a crisis of identity. Not the kind that's so serious I don't know who I am. What I mean is, I've been forced to work out who I'm working for while the boss is away. (I like calling him the boss. It makes me feel I'm being subservient.)

He had only been away for a few days before I had spent countless hours chasing round to photocopy more than a hundred copies each of three different leaflets. There were notice sheets which are given out each week in church; there were tickets for a special men's meeting; and finally there were questionnaires for each person to fill in about the parish weekend.

But my work didn't stop with the photocopying itself. I then had to sort the papers into piles, name them, and deliver the piles to the folk who'd agreed to distribute them. Phew!

Tom was at the fifth house I visited to deliver the wretched leaflets. By the time I arrived I was a bit flustered. In fact, as I look back on it, I can see that I was

probably in one of those obnoxious super-efficient must-get-this-done moods.

Tom wasn't. Indeed, it became quite obvious from the moment he opened the door that he was feeling decidedly laid-back.

I had hardly said hello before I was thrusting pages into his hands and relaying instructions from the boss.

Tom stepped back and leaned nonchalantly against his front-door post. 'What ye doin'?' he asked in his strong Lancashire accent.

I stopped for a second and looked at him.

'I'm giving you these notice sheets for the service tomorrow,' I replied. 'It's my "supportive vicar's wife" role, if you hadn't noticed.'

'Oh yeah?' Tom scratched his head, as if to take things in, but everything about him remained decidedly unimpressed. Then he smiled musingly. 'You look very busy at it anyway, Jane.'

At that moment I did not appreciate being analysed. Quickly I retorted, 'So would you, Tom, if you had spent the last two hours chasing round the place for your boss!'

If it hadn't been Tom, I might have thought that he expected the vicar's wife to do this sort of thing devotedly all day long. But I knew that Tom is well aware of how much work goes on behind the scenes, and he had always been kind and supportive. Suddenly, as I stood back from his doorstep, I saw myself from his perspective: I was no more than a flurry of activity. His laid-back approach was in such contrast that I stood back and laughed at myself.

'The things I do for the vicar!' I joked.

But as soon as I had said it, I stopped.

'Oh no,' I corrected. 'I'm not doing it for the vicar, am I?'

It was a question really. 'I'm doing it for you lot, aren't I? This is all for you parishioners.'

Tom's quiet smile only grew. 'I suppose that's right really,' he chuckled.

Indignation rose within me. 'Right,' I began again, 'in that case, you'd better jolly well not forget to give out these, and these, and these, or I'll crown you!'

'Oh yeah?' Tom looked just as bemused and uninterested as before.

'Yeah,' I said as assertively as I could.

But for all our joking, as I drove home my own thoughts about that conversation lingered on. Who had I done all that running around for? Was it the vicar? Or the parishioners? Or was it even for God? Because if that was the case, then I really ought to have been a lot more willing and cheerful about it.

There was plenty to pray about that night. But I'm still glad that our holiday starts tomorrow.

31   The Parish Strikes Back

26th August

While the cat's away, the mice will play. During our fortnight in Spain, my friends Mabel (alias Marmaduke's wife, in italics) and Sarah grabbed the microphones of BBC Radio Merseyside.

We've been reprieved. She's away – the vicar's wife, I mean. You know, that Jane Grayshon.

And we, as parishioners, thought this was an opportunity not to be missed. We thought we could put you right on a few things.

Not 'The Empire Strikes Back', but 'The Parish Strikes Back'.

Where shall we start?

Why do you turn on your radio each Sunday morning? Does she make you laugh? Do you enjoy what she says?

Our motivation for listening is quite different. Self-preservation, it's called. We wait with fear and trepidation. Will we recognise ourselves behind those false names?

Or, did I really do that?

You see, if Albert's at church, there's the 10.30 am post-mortem on what the vicar's wife said and about whom. If we're going to deny all knowledge with any conviction, we have to listen. And anyone can tell who has.

There are those who smile.

She was nice about them.

And those who are rather quiet.

She was less restrained about them.

Where does she find the things to say? From us, of course! If you ever come to one of our church services, don't be fooled by seeing Jane, busily taking notes on the sermon. She may be...

But there's another page, headed in capital letters, 'BBC VW.'

That is, 'BBC vicar's wife.'

At one meeting she sat next to me with three sheets of paper on her knee. One for any good points the speaker made, one for thank-you letters she owed, and one for vicar's wife anecdotes. And somehow she managed to keep flicking between all three at once; her brain manages to keep several different strands of thought flowing simultaneously.

We keep thinking, or rather hoping, that she's going to run out of stories. But alas, no. They keep coming, week after week. We're never safe.

And as for her memory...

Just because you didn't hear your tale this week, there's always next week.

Or next month.

Or even possibly next year.

As the films always say, 'What you say has been taken down and may be used as evidence against you.'

But actually Jane is concerned whether we're enjoying life or whether we're finding things hard. She's genuinely interested and she always listens when we need to talk.

A bit like God, really. He accepts us, just as we are.

The thing is, we can't give you one picture that says it all. She is certainly quite a character.

But then if you tune in every week I suppose you know that.

There are so many sides to her; just when you think you've got her taped, you see yet another aspect of her personality.

We got a different view of her at our parish weekend. Do you remember?

How could I forget?

Picture the scene: Jane plus sundry children standing in the grounds of a big old house next to a field full of cows. The children wanted the cows to come closer, so Jane –

Being Jane –

Said she would fix it for them. She leaned over the wall...

Bottom in the air...

And started snorting, much to everyone's entertainment.

And, believe it or not, the cows came right up close and snorted back! She did look funny, nose to nose with a big black and white cow. I wish I'd had my camera to catch the view from behind.

Well, as Albert says, Body Beautiful is in sunny Spain now. Life has been harrowing for her recently so we hope that Spain refreshes those parts that even Whiston Hospital didn't get to. And you can have her back next week.

32   One Figleaf or Three?

2nd September

So... they tried to get at me behind my back, did they? The Parish Strikes Back indeed. But, ha ha, it didn't work because the producer broadcast their (no doubt) slanderous stuff about me unusually early, so lots of people missed it. They tuned in at 8:25, only to hear the final music fading into the distance. I take this as proof that God is on my side after all – making sure that tasteless stories about me were not heard by everyone!

In the meantime, we've had a great holiday with no telephone and no doorbell. And the ultimate bliss: we could even go to the supermarket without anyone peering into our shopping trolley to get a glimpse of what vicars buy (yes, we do need toilet rolls). We could totally forget that Matthew was a vicar.

Except twice.

The first time was on the beach. Somehow we got talking (or, I should say, listening) to a rather loud lady with an unfortunate mega-voice. The whole conversation thus got relayed across the beach – where were we from? How long were we staying? What did we do?

'Oh, you're a *vicar*, are you? A man of the cloth?' She laughed a little nervously.

Half the females within a radius of 100 yards suddenly put their tops on. It was a bit reminiscent of Adam and Eve covering themselves in the Garden of Eden... though, come to think of it, we're not told, are we, whether Eve had one figleaf or three?

The second occasion was at a barbeque at a nearby villa. The other three men, who had all made a lot of money working in the motor trade, were enjoying a somewhat ribald conversation. About halfway through the evening someone made the mistake of asking Matthew what he did for a living.

You should've seen their faces! At first they refused to believe him and Matthew had to repeat about eight times that he truly wasn't having them on. Even then they turned to me for verification. I don't think that helped them actually. I simply grinned and asked with a shrug of my shoulders, 'Can't you tell? Don't you think I look the image of a vicar's wife?' Somehow that made them even more confused.

They were quite twitchy for a while (until they'd had more wine), trying to explain away all the 'relaxed' language and stories they had previously been regaling us with. It all seemed so silly to me. Who did they think they were kidding? Matthew? Or God? I wished they knew how forgiving God is.

The man I felt most sorry for was sitting right next to me. His jaw had dropped about half a mile as horror struck. It was as if he had bumped into his own conscience for the first time in ages and his reaction was clearly a pleading, 'Please go away! I'm on holiday!'

I was going to lean across and reassure him that it really was OK; that Matthew's nice and God's even nicer, but that seemed a bit heavy for holiday barbeque chatter. So instead I just beamed at him and offered him another lamb chop. I hoped he might get the message anyway.

I wish we weren't brought up always to ask what people do for a living.

I've heard of a much better idea to talk about on holiday. You tell everyone you're on honeymoon.

It works wonders. Everyone is really nice to you, and if you're lucky they give you free drinks as well. It's true! It was friends who first told us this ploy – *after* we came home from our real honeymoon, when we'd been too shy to tell anyone. We had obviously missed out, they said, and told us we should take the opportunity to use the tactic next holiday instead. They thoroughly recommended it after several years' repetition.

You'd have to be careful not to go back two years running to the same hotel with the same story. At least, not with the same spouse.

33 How Can God Let this Happen?

9th September

They do say, don't they, that coming back from holiday is like descending to earth with a bump. This week has been no exception for us. I've just learned that my friend Violet's son Mark is ill, living on a knife-edge.

Why do I mention him, when I don't go into detail about every parishioner's ailment? I'll tell you why.

You can go on and on in this job, taking phone calls and doing visits, meeting people and hearing about things that go wrong in their lives. Mostly you cope with the grief; it's a bit like when I was nursing really, where other people's suffering had to be categorised as 'work', so that it didn't drag each nurse down all the time. But then sometimes you get caught off guard, and a situation hits you right between the eyes.

Mark is one such example. He's just seven, and while we were away he went to the doctor, had some tests, and very quickly had to have a very serious operation on his brain.

Mark had been in hospital for a week before Matthew

and I came home from holiday. In one sense that made it hard for us actually, because we felt we had let the family down. We would have wanted to be alongside them in their worry, and pray with them. And it also hurts more because Mark is a child, and in this country we get more upset over children suffering. Everyone says (to themselves if not out loud), 'Aah, he's so little and innocent.'

And then they ask the question that bugs so many people; it's the question which stops them from wanting to come near to God. Ever. 'How can God let this happen?' they ask. They assume he must be a nasty, uncaring God.

If the vicar's wife is lucky, people will not only express that sort of emotion behind her back. They will not be frightened that it's the 'wrong thing to say'. They will say it to her face, and it becomes a sincere question.

I am lucky. Within a few hours of getting back last week, Violet's husband had come to talk; next day I saw Violet. And my heart – and Matthew's – felt as heavy as theirs as we shared with them in the seriousness of all that is wrong with Mark.

It would be so easy to dole out platitudes. It would be easy to say, 'Never mind, I'll pray for you, and God loves us all anyway.' But personally I don't think that's helpful. The fact is that we don't know the whole answer to the big question, 'Why?' And for Christians to give glib answers merely serves to keep people at a safe distance, and to protect us from the pain of caring deeply.

And so all this week, although I've been refreshed by that wonderful holiday, I have had a heavy heart. What could I do? Go and see them, yes, occasionally. But not for long, because they're all weary and they've had enough of visitors staying too long.

I have prayed. Oh, how I've prayed! No speeches, because I don't know what to say to God. All *I* want to ask is for him to make Mark better, but I don't know if he'll do that. So I've used the prayers in the Psalms: one of them seemed particularly meaningful. It asks God if there's something wrong, because he seems so uncompassionate. But it does end by saying, 'I will remember the good things you've done, and I'll think about those, and I'll trust you to be nice like that again.'

There are admittedly some good things. Mark himself is absolutely fantastic. He is being so brave, he is in amazingly good spirits. And his mum says she feels very peaceful; she knows God is with her. It's an inspiration to see her.

Perhaps one of the jobs we can do is to tell people that, and allow others to see where God *is* at work, even if he is not doing what we all want.

Meanwhile, I'll get back to square one, learning how to pray.

34　　　　　　　　　A General Dog's Body

16th September

We have what is called the Thanksgiving service in church this Sunday. It's a day when we pledge back to God our gifts of time and money.

In preparation, each of us has been handed a green card to fill in which offers a huge list of suggestions as to what we might give. Read the lesson, lead the prayers, be a sidesperson, teach Sunday School, change nappies at the crêche, join a home group, sew banners.... Nobody at our place can complain of being confined to cleaning or arranging flowers!

The paragraph which caught my eye is at the end of the card. It says, 'Please feel free to add anything we have missed – maybe something that you are doing already.'

What an opportunity! The question is, 'How on earth can I sum everything up in three meagre lines?'

For the first line, I think I'll put, 'Being a shock absorber,' because I do feel expected to absorb all the complaints and moans about what people dislike in church. Some folk seem to imagine that if they have a quiet word with the smiling vicar's wife, she can work on the vicar. As if I'd want to ruin intimate moments with my husband by introducing *that* sort of talk! Such a prospect is worse than cleaning bedpans in my nursing days.

Then on the second line I might put, 'Being a general dog's body.' Doing all those little jobs which don't count in themselves, but which mount up in a vicarage because they happen all the time. For example, 'Do you think you could possibly fold all these leaflets for me, darling?' Or, *dring dring*, ''Scuse me, could ya tache a message for the vichar?' Or, 'Darling – ' (that endearment always bodes trouble) ' – this is the only chance I have to see so-and-so. Could the meal be an hour later?' (when the soufflé has just risen to perfection).

I shouldn't moan. Whenever I sink to that, I reveal an unwillingness for which I pray God will forgive me. I do want to be a cheerful giver.

Mind you, being a dog's body can be pretty literal. Occasionally we look after pets for people who are away. We once had one who was so lively that whenever I took him to the parkland, I ended up tethering him to a washing line with the other end around my waist. A brilliant idea, I thought.

I had clearly not anticipated the consequences.

When the dog saw a lady dog about half a mile away, he shot off at top speed in hot pursuit. With smug innocence I thought to myself, 'You're going to regret this, dog!'

Seconds later the coils of rope ran out, and my smile disappeared. I was suddenly jerked up into the air, like a glider on take-off. I have no idea how far I flew. All recollections were blotted out by the thud of my landing. As I slowed, I was dragged for the final yards right through a cow pat.

A man who had been walking nearby rushed over to me. I felt so humiliated that I began to wish I had been knocked unconscious by the fall. All this, just to be kind to someone! Sometimes I feel exactly like a dog's body.

The third line of my green form will be the easiest. I suspect it may be the most important bit of being a vicar's wife. It's certainly the nicest.

I shall write, 'Giving cuddles to a harassed vicar.'

That one comes naturally.

35 The Making of a Movie: Concealing Crossed Wires

23rd September

Our house has been bugged. It began with a telephone call a couple of months ago: would I be willing to be the subject of a documentary on television? They wanted to illustrate my first book, *A Pathway through Pain*. Ooh yes. I felt honoured; excited. And I cannot deny that a bit of pride probably crept into my reactions.

But as the interviews and phone calls increased – and this was still weeks before any filming began – I began to realise that glamour is but one part of the work. Whereas I used to think of a documentary as a window on to someone's life, I would now describe it as more like a door, through which countless people march in and take over.

There were six members of the crew who seemed to live in our house for weeks. The cameraman and the sound recordist's jobs were obvious. Someone else was responsible for the lighting – he had spotlights on stands, and those umbrella things to reflect the light, and filters to change the colouring. Then there was the researcher who had to make sure everybody was ready at the right time, and the production assistant who made endless cups of coffee to keep us all sweet... especially the director, who was the Boss Man. We all did whatever he said.

Between them, they and their equipment were strewn all over the house. Thus it seemed a little farcical when they filmed me playing the piano to demonstrate how I relax. I had tripped over the yards of wire on my way across the room to reach the piano itself. I was

surrounded by lights, cameras, tripod, microphone and monitor, and as if all that was not enough, the lights became so hot that after a while the smoke alarm in the hall started to ring – right in the middle of my Beethoven piece!

When the time came for us to be filmed eating a meal, we invited the minister and his wife Rachel to join us. Matthew had given himself the position of chief watchdog on the alert for any pretentiousness on my part. On that day he decreed loftily, 'We'll have soup and rolls and fruit. No more!'

So much for my idea of a fantastic cordon bleu meal concocted with great panache as if I cooked like that every day. Had that been so very wrong?

However, Matthew is the head of the household, so soup and rolls and fruit was the menu.

It was when Rachel was stretching her hand towards a nice juicy orange that the sound man started flapping his hand in a gesture of increasing urgency. Soon the director joined in from behind the camera, shaking his head and mouthing, 'Don't touch the fruit!'

It transpired that a microphone had been hidden in the fruit bowl – perched behind an apple – and, had Rachel taken the orange, she would have revealed the wire. Such a revelation would apparently have been considered indecent on television.

They went to enormous lengths to be discreet, the cost of which is totally lost on most viewers. Within a few minutes of their arrival on the very first day, for example, the sound man was investigating my blouse to see how easily he could hide his microphone. He surmised that a clip would not be suitable, and that he should instead fasten a tiny microphone to my skin, about six inches below my chin.

I schooled my imagination not to run riot. In steady silence I watched him pass the tiny, cold wire down the front of my blouse. It soon became obvious that the trickiest bit was to be when he tried to catch the end of that wire from below.

'Just think of my hands as the hands of a doctor,' he said with a calm smile which was intended to reassure me. What he did not realise was that, while he spoke, there was a doctor waiting in the wings who was to be included in the film; and not just any old doctor, but my friend Marmaduke!

I prayed that Marmaduke would have closed his ears to such comments from the sound man.

'There,' he said, securing the tape to my skin and refastening the button, 'embarrassment over: you can go. From now on I'll be able to hear every sound you make, wherever you go.'

As I walked away, I sensed that my embarrassment was only just beginning. Most pressingly, I wished that I had visited the loo *before* being wired to his earphones.

36 The Making of a Movie: Taking Temperatures the French Way

30th September

It's not every day that you get the chance to be wheeled along on one of those theatre trolleys with another man. You may know how narrow those hospital trolleys are; and the sides were folded up, which meant we really were snuggled together.

The other man was, of course, the cameraman who, happily for me, was the best-looking of the whole crew. Oh, we did have some laughs, especially with the hospital scenes. Perhaps the laughter dissipated the underlying emotion of grief in recalling the awfulness of my collapse in April.

We had to reconstruct my being rushed into Casualty at Whiston Hospital. The film director – who must be obeyed – had directed the porter to take me, looking unconscious in a wheelchair, towards a cubicle and behind a curtain, as if I were being admitted. The most difficult task fell to the cameraman who had to race backwards at top speed in front of the wheelchair, without falling over.

In Take One we hurtled towards the nearest cubicle and drew back the curtain, only to be confronted by three of the crew hiding in there, pointing through their giggles for us to go to the next cubicle along.

Take Two. I took the opportunity, then, to ask the question which had been bothering me for weeks beforehand: what on earth was I supposed to look like in this scene? Marmaduke and Mabel could both recall the actual hospital admission equally vividly.

'Dead,' said Marmaduke. 'You looked dead.'

I thanked him emptily and turned to Mabel for a more helpful answer. How could I look dead? This was not acting, it was reconstructing reality; so how, exactly, did I look?

'Slumped,' she answered, echoing her husband's monosyllabic reply. But then she added, 'Just go slumped in your chair. Here, you relax and I'll do it for you.' She pushed my head forwards. There, thankfully, my facial expression was hidden.

People have asked us, 'What did your neighbours think of all this activity around the vicarage?' Well, I'm afraid I don't know. I haven't dared ask. What if any of them noticed the director one Thursday standing at the front door while the cameraman parked his van, and they overheard him call out, 'We'll do the bedroom scene now'? They might not have realised that that scene was to pose one of the greatest problems for me: how could I pretend to be asleep without dissolving into laughter?

I tried my very hardest. I tried to think of serious and solemn things. But of course, being me, I got the giggles. Three times. In fact, the editor has stuck all such 'out-takes' on video – the sort that Dennis Norden enjoys. The best shot on that video was filmed in the chapel of a theological college. The camera spanned round the congregation until it focused on the principal. At exactly the moment he came into the centre of the screen, he picked his ear; and then the camera panned back.

The moral of that must be, 'Pick your moment.'

But the crew weren't out to show up anyone in a bad way. On the contrary. For one scene they even used a special filter. They said it was to 'add a touch of softness'. I am under no illusion that they meant I had a spot on my chin that day. I gather there's one famous actress who doesn't allow television cameras to come nearer than a certain number of metres without a filter lens. She refuses to be seen as she is. I can't say I agree with that philosophy. After all, it may not be very complimentary, but there's no filter between ourselves and God, is there? He sees us as we are. *Au naturel.*

Which brings me back to the final scene in the hospital. A nurse was to take my temperature and the director wanted to calculate the best angle for the shot. He asked the nurse, 'Would you always take a temperature that way?'

For a moment I thought he was questioning whether the thermometer might be inserted elsewhere – the vet's way.

Quick as a flash I answered for her. 'I am not having my temperature taken any other way.'

Just then I remembered that the director's wife is French. His eyes lit up as he considered aloud, 'In France, you know, they don't take your temperature like this...'

But I refused to do things the French way. There are some things over which even a gentle vicar's wife will put her foot down.

37   Our God Rains

7th October

My landing back on earth from Cloud Nine was rather jerky. It came after all the filming for the documentary was over; on an evening when I was totally buoyed up by nice remarks.

I had addressed a large meeting in the Wirral. Several 'fans' came up enthusiastically afterwards, giving my old morale a real boost. It was probably all quite unreal, I know, but it made me feel great while the glow lasted.

Which was about fifteen minutes after I had left.

By that time I was on the motorway driving home, alone. And if there's one memorable aspect of that particular evening, it is that it was raining. Not just a little drizzle. It was absolutely pouring down with saturating, drenching rain. And I ran out of petrol.

Before any man makes a rude or chauvinistic comment, I might point out that this was not my fault! The petrol gauge had gone on strike, but Matthew had assured me there was another fifty miles' worth in the tank, so I took his word for it. The mistake of his assessment only became evident when the car spluttered to an ungainly halt.

I stared through the windscreen at the wet blackness. There was only blackness. And I realised with a sigh that my only 'coat' was my smart designer jacket. Moreover, it was black. To wear it on my plod to the emergency telephone would amount to little less than suicide. There was no choice but to shed it and wear only my skimpy but white blouse. At least that would be seen.

I had walked only a few paces before I knew I had come down to earth. Because there's no doubt about it: walking along in the rain with a thin blouse at a quarter to midnight in total darkness, having showers flung at you at high speed from lorries hugging the side of the motorway, is a very effective counterbalance for someone whose head has become a bit swollen with compliments.

I was unable to see any puddles until I was in them. They were so cold, I reached the stage where I stopped draining the water out of my shoes. I thought maybe if I left it in it might warm up a little.

The motorway police, when I phoned for help, told me to return to my car but not to get in. 'It's too dangerous to sit in a car on a hard shoulder,' they said.

'In *this* weather?' I asked, but the wind was so loud I could not hear their reply.

I made my way to a nearby bridge which I hoped would provide at least some shelter. Vain hope! The particular bridge I had chosen had a leak. As I stood there waiting for my devoted husband to come to my aid – bless him – I became aware of a steady trickle of water splashing down right beside me.

Now, the evening's programme earlier had included refreshments and I had enjoyed three cups of tea with my biscuits. Very nice, you may say. Yes, but I jolly well regretted that third cuppa when I heard the sound of that trickling stream splashing beside me. I looked round for a bush, but in vain. All I could do was cross my legs.

That must have been the point when I became past caring. Abandoning myself completely to the ridicule of the whole situation, I suddenly I heard myself singing. At the top of my voice, to drown the din of the thundering, water-chucking traffic – and the trickle from above – I sang. 'This is the day that the Lord has made.'

It might have been more appropriate to sing, 'Our God reigns.'

And then I began to laugh and laugh. I had heard of 'giving thanks in all circumstances', but this was not far from insanity.

Still, I could thank God for finding such a colourful way of knocking me off my pedestal and putting me in my rightful place!

But, er, I'd hate to think that nobody will say complimentary things ever again.

38   No Reading Matter

14th October

I suspect that I have become unguardedly oblivious as to how vicar-ish and strange some aspects of my life are to normal people.

I am thinking at the moment about the books that Matthew reads.

We travelled by train to London recently and I thought nothing of the fact that Matthew was reading a book about funerals. It was called something like, 'Funerals and how to survive them', or, perhaps, 'Funerals and how to improve them'. I did not bat an eyelid. I had my own reading material: a very interesting biography of a guy with AIDS. I was preparing an interview about it on radio.

At Crewe the train filled up and every seat became occupied. A strong perfume came to sit next to Matthew with a blonde girl carrying it. She didn't seem terribly respectful of the distance between them – she rather snuggled up to him, actually. I might say, he wasn't wearing his Ring of Confidence dog collar.

You should have seen her face when Matthew got up to buy a sandwich, because of course he laid down his book on the table as he went, didn't he? The title shouted in large letters the word 'FUNERALS'. From her previous bored and glazed expression, suddenly this girl's eyes widened. She looked questioningly across towards me, but clearly that only made things much worse for her. The front of my book had 'AIDS' plastered across it.

When Matthew returned I secretly watched the reflection in the window. His blonde neighbour endeavoured to read surreptitiously over his shoulder. She kept squinting to her left and her eye muscles were working such overtime it was like callanetics for eyes! Between his book and mine she must have concluded that one of us had AIDS and we were making early preparations for the funeral.

I couldn't help seeing the episode as a picture of what happens so often in the life of a vicar. People see him doing something, or saying something, which they don't quite understand and they get hold of completely the wrong end of the stick... like church services which seem like absolute mumbo-jumbo to some folk, but they rarely ask what's going on, or why.

We've had some very friendly chats with some builders working next door to us at the moment. One of them told me, 'When we were younger, we would never have talked to a vicar like we do with Matthew. We'd never think of just calling at a vicarage as so many people do to you!'

'Why not?' I asked.

For a long minute they thought. 'It's your conscience,' they laughed.

I wish we all believed as strongly in forgiveness as we do in shame. Then we would feel free to chat to God much more easily than we do.

Still, I've been browsing along Matthew's bookshelves to find good titles for our next train journey – for the entertainment of those next to us.

How about *The Big Sin*? Especially if it were accompanied by *I'm OK – You're OK*.

But if Matthew took *Crisis in Masculinity*, or, *Marriage Without Pretending,* I'm not sure that I'd sit in the same carriage.

39   Peanuts: Salted or Roasted?

21st October

On Monday evening I met with the editor of my next book, to talk informally over a drink.

The fact that we've become friends was proved when our initial politeness – taking one peanut at a time – did not last long. The fourth time they were offered, Henry ripped the packet open.

'I'm sorry, but I like to relish the taste of these things,' he said. 'So, if you don't mind, I'll take a handful of them at once.' He poured them into the palm of his hand and flicked them straight into his mouth.

'Here – do join me,' he said. Enthusiastically he poured some into my own hand.

With a sideways glance I tried to copy his flick, tipping them all onto my tongue. Unfortunately, I wasn't well practised and, when my head was back, one peanut missed my mouth.

Suddenly I regretted wearing a rather low-cut dress. The peanut had simply disappeared.

So had my smile. I looked down, hoping against all hope that it might have gone onto my lap.

It hadn't.

'It didn't miss, did it?' Henry enquired graciously. I think he felt faintly responsible for his failed lesson in 'How to Eat Peanuts by the Handful'.

I looked up to see in Henry's face a mixture of sympathy and ... well, I can only describe it as hope.

I replied uncomfortably, 'It didn't exactly miss...'

For a moment I was suspended between a blushing embarrassment and a rising desire to give way to a fit of giggles. The slight twitch of his dark moustache heralded helpless laughter between us.

When it had subsided, we resumed our discussion. I knew it was time, then, for me to suppress the urgent instinct to deal with the wretched thing. Etiquette dictates that one mustn't do that: especially not if you're a vicar's wife. This was a meeting with my publisher: informal, but still a business meeting. I must not wriggle. I must concentrate on the matter in hand... not the matter in my clothes.

It was almost impossible. My mind kept coming back to the offending little piece which was by then beginning to itch.

I remembered the story of a politician who, when dining with the Queen, had dropped a roast potato on the floor. As he was endeavouring to kick it discreetly to one side, Her Majesty had caught his eye and commented, 'Life can be awfully trying at times.'

That hour with Henry seemed awfully trying, too. I began to wonder about famous people whom we see on television having really important conversations. Despite their confident and smiling exterior, how often are they struggling to hide the fact that something is wrong underneath? Like a peanut down the wrong place?

How often during our conversations with God, are we desperately trying to hide the fact that something is all wrong underneath? Something which presses in on us, even while we appear to be fine and we pretend that all is well?

It only took a second, but I cannot say too strongly that the relief was wonderful when I fished out that peanut.

I stuck it to a blank card and posted it to Henry.

40   Out of the Mouths of Children

28th October

On Tuesday morning last week, the builders, who were still working next door, whistled across as I walked by.

'Just a minute, darling!' they called. 'We've brought a present for you! It's a packet of peanuts...'

That was but the first of many – thank you – along with comments which I shall not repeat.

In fact so many people have mentioned peanuts to me or Matthew this week, including those right up in the church hierarchy who I did not know listened, that I think I should take the opportunity on this programme to point out some of the good things we do.

For example, Matthew and I try very hard to give a welcome to other people, and that's not because Matthew is a vicar. In fact, in the good old days when we got married, when Matthew was normal (a teacher and not a vicar), one of the readings we chose for our wedding was about 'welcoming others' and 'practising hospitality'.

Nowadays, however, we are at a distinct disadvantage

because there's an off-putting sign on our house saying 'Vicarage'. (Anyone would think it said 'Dentist' from the way people seem so terrified of opening their mouths in front of us.)

Mind you, that's not everyone. To my dying day I shall never forget a lady many years ago. She sat in the garden talking to Matthew, her voice so loud that I think all the neighbours must have overheard her side of the conversation with quite some fascination.

The excerpt which I heard was, 'Of course, *I* don't commit adultery... or at least, only a little.'

There was a pause while Matthew spoke (I later learned he was asking what she meant by 'a little adultery').

'Only on Fridays,' she said.

I don't know about our neighbours, but at that point I certainly decided I must go out to the shops.

A second way of helping people to feel at ease with us is to share a meal with them. Marmaduke and Mabel are great at reciprocating invitations and not long ago, when her parents were staying there, they invited our whole family along for lunch.

Mabel's father looked terribly nervous of the vicar. He talked almost incessantly, making jokes or saying anything to distract himself from his anxiety.

By the end of the first course he had had a couple of glasses of wine and had loosened up a little. Suddenly, out slipped a word which he hadn't intended; the sort of word which you would really try not to say in front of a vicar.

He covered his mouth as if to stopper it up.

'Ooh, ooh I am sorry,' he giggled nervously, eyeing Matthew with apprehension. 'I shouldn't say these things in front of the children.'

Angus, who is eight, was sitting next to him and he put down his knife and fork. 'It's all right,' he said calmly.

I felt very proud of the way our son had obviously learned to put people at their ease. I smiled encouragingly across to him.

'It's all right,' he went on. 'My daddy sometimes says, "******".'

Does anyone, anywhere, manage a good impression of themselves *and* be honest? Or can only God do that?

41

Should I Have Called You 'Doctor'?

4th November

'Yes, I'm still working,' called one of the builders as he climbed his ladder on to next door's roof.

I quickly gathered he was quoting from what I said about him last week. I was surprised he had listened.

'Oh yes,' he answered. 'Your audience must have gone up since my wife and I started listening.'

At that moment Matthew joined us. 'Her ratings may have gone up,' he said, 'but my reputation must be going down!'

Poor man. It must be easier for vicars whose wives don't pull them down a peg or two. They can stay on their pedestals. But at least God didn't stay on a pedestal: he came down to our level and became utterly human.

This week our builder didn't stop to chat. He was under the eaves by now. 'I've got to work one to one ratio on this bit; and I have to do it quickly before it goes off,' he shouted down. 'It's hard going!'

As we stepped back into the house I whispered to Matthew that phrases about ratios and stuff meant nothing to me. It was jargon.

Matthew explained that he was referring to roof mortar which apparently has to be extra strong. Then he mused, 'I think I could use exactly those words to describe my work, you know. I have "got to work one to one" telling the Good News. I have to be quick or they "go off"! And that's pretty hard going, too!'

I happened to know what Matthew meant, but I did wonder how many people outside his 'trade' would understand him.

Which led me to think how peculiar we humans are in the way we use words. We sit and laugh at television films with imaginary beings from outer space talking made-up jargon, but every trade or profession has its own language. What's the difference between that and how we use incomprehensible words?

I once challenged a man who came to look at our gas-boiler. The only explanation he gave me at first was, 'It's broken.' Nothing more. And when I asked him *what* had broken, he looked heavenwards, as if to exclaim, 'You're a woman, dear: you'll never understand this!' And then, instead of explaining helpfully, he proceeded to get all technical (I'm sure he picked the most obscure words he could think of) about heat exchangers and coils and ratios.

I interrupted him. 'Hang on a minute,' I said, 'I don't understand that.'

He gave a triumphant smile; then in a condescending tone he replied – as if innocently – 'You asked me to explain...'

I was not going to be beaten like that. 'Listen: I could explain to *you* all about vasectomies, but if you were

having one done I suspect you would be much more interested to hear how the operation will affect you, than any talk of forceps and ligatures and the size of the scalpel blade.'

He turned decidedly green. Satisfied, I stopped. I had made my point.

Well, why use silly words if they prevent other people from understanding the message?

Which was exactly what I thought the next time I

went to church and, unusually, we had the really old-fashioned service. Beautiful words, but jargon to all those who'd never learned old English. Two teenagers, newcomers to church, even went out giggling as if they thought we were from outer space. Shouldn't we have been helping them to understand?

Incidentally, the plumber telephoned me on the evening of his visit. He was exceptionally nice.

'I feel I owe you an apology,' he said pleasantly. 'Should I have called you "Doctor"?'

His conclusion demonstrated that not only are vicars' wives undervalued: midwives are as well.

42

It Shouldn't Happen to an Osteopath

11th November

I awoke on Monday morning to find that my back had seized up overnight. Having once injured a disc, this time I knew to make an immediate appointment with the osteopath.

My half-hour session began with me sitting on the couch, dressed like Eve. He stood behind me, probing gently around the vertebrae; and when he reached my neck I voiced my fear that maybe I had caused the pain myself. Maybe I had strained it working for so long at the computer, in my endeavour to complete the manuscript of my book.

'Oh?' he sounded interested. 'What is this book called?' He took hold of my arms and, one by one, he crossed them over my chest.

'It's called, *The Confessions of a Vicar's Wife*,' I replied.

He roared with laughter. 'That's a good one!' he said.

I silently watched him place a cushion between my

arms and chest. Still from behind, he put his arms around me, encircling me until he could clasp each elbow, whereupon he pulled me close to him and rocked me. I tried to swallow my apprehension and relax into the swaying motion.

'Perhaps I should write a book, too,' he speculated, 'and call it "It Shouldn't Happen to an Osteopath".'

Suddenly he gave one strong, thrusting jerk which reverberated right down my spine. I heard a loud involuntary grunt as all my breath was pushed from my lungs.

This shouldn't happen to a vicar's wife, I thought.

'That's good,' he said, satisfied. I was not invited to disagree. He turned me on to one side and began a rather more soothing massage, replacing my bewildered silence with an ambling conversation as if nothing unusual had happened.

'The trouble with fiction – and I presume your book is fiction – '

His pummelling across my shoulder blades left me so winded that I could not catch my breath to answer, 'No, it isn't.'

'... is that characters from real life must creep into your imaginary stories. Do they?'

Little did he know how near the bone he was; that his very conversation was providing me with the sort of subject material on which I rely.

Blithely he continued, 'Where d'you do the research, then, to find out what life is like for a vicar's wife?'

It was some minutes later when he turned me towards him that I had time to admit that my book is not fiction, and that I have no need to research it nor even look beyond my own everyday life.

'Go on with you!' he said; but when he heard my innocent assurances, his protest soon gave way to suspicion and, eventually, acceptance that I was telling the truth.

He became very subdued. He asked me how my Confessions started, and I told him about my work on radio. I became quite animated, then, sharing the fun of my experiences behind the scenes of local BBC.

'It's not every woman who can come home to her husband and announce gleefully that she's done a good day's work in the red light area!' I told him rather impishly.

He froze for a second, as shocked as if I had winded him.

'You know,' I assured him quickly, 'outside a studio. There's always a red light to indicate when you're "on the air".'

He listened with intrigue while I went on to tell how, before any recording starts, the presenter is asked to 'give a bit of level'.

'You wot?' you think, when you first hear the phrase. 'A bit of level?'

What they mean is that they want to hear you say something – anything – so that they can adjust the dials according to your voice. But in order to avoid details the producer quite often says, 'Just tell me what you had for breakfast.'

Well, one week I had had twelve clergymen for breakfast. (What a thing to wake up to!) The local group of them meet once a month at seven o'clock in the morning to have communion together, followed by breakfast at each other's homes. Matthew says they usually get cereal and cold leathery toast. So I decided to go to town. The way to a man's heart and all that. I had steaming hot porridge ready for them, followed by fresh coffee with toast and a full cooked breakfast. I even included devilled kidneys.

Mind you, after my story about devilled kidneys when I was nursing, I don't know if anyone will ever touch kidneys again.

Time forbade my telling the osteopath about that one, but on reflection, I think I said quite sufficient for one day.

The gnawing fear which pressed on my mind as I left him was that one day that osteopath might write his book; and he might tell a story of an outrageous broadcaster who claimed to be a vicar's wife.

43 Inclusive Language

18th November

My husband had to chair a tricky meeting last Wednesday. All members of the church had been invited to come and air their views on inclusive language.

'What language?' you might ask. Inclusive language. You know, watch what you say in case you offend the females. You must have heard the sort of thing: the 'Everyman' theatre in Liverpool now has to be referred to as the 'Everyperson' theatre; and one gets embroiled in all sorts of complicated messes trying to rephrase words like 'manager' or 'brinkmanship'.

Matthew brought the matter to our attention because, as he pointed out, the church doesn't need to be hundreds of years behind the times on everything. So, what did we all think of the words we use in church?

I felt in a slightly tricky situation actually, because I held the opposite view to Matthew. But how can a vicar's wife express disagreement diplomatically? I didn't want to lead a counter-revolution against my beloved!

Unpredictably, it was Matthew who was advocating change to give women a better deal. He was very gentle.

'Can't you hear,' he explained patiently, 'that I cause some women to feel left out if I stand and pronounce, "We have sinned against God and against our fellow *men*"? It's not just the men who are involved.'

Yes, I see that. But I've never felt left out myself, so I couldn't argue strongly about it.

There were those who definitely did not want anything changed at all. And there were those who were all for changing everything – every last word.

Like Rachel. She sat on the edge of her chair pulling her sleeves up when she began to speak, as if she were all set to get stuck in.

'Should we change the name of the Manse?' she asked eagerly.

You could go on... How do we talk about God's 'manifold' blessings? Or that he 'manifested' himself?

Actually, nobody thought the Bible itself should be altered, although Marmaduke pointed out the most strongly exclusive passages such as the description of 'manna' in the desert. Songs seemed to be different, though – especially Christmas carols. What about 'Good Christian men rejoice' or 'Born that man no more should die'? Do they exclude women?

But if you go that far, you would have to ban the word 'hymns'. And 'Amen'.

I shouldn't mock. At least, not exclusively so. Because beneath the fun there is a thread of serious thought. The angels didn't mean, 'Peace on earth, goodwill towards men.' God's peace and goodwill are towards everybody.

If we'll listen, of course.

And the Bible doesn't mean, 'Man shall live by bread alone.' (Though seeing how quickly some men get through my home baking does make me wonder.) No, it means that all of us hunger for deeper things in life; we all hunger for God.

If only we'd admit it.

I don't know about you, but personally I've always felt those Bible promises do include me. So I'm quite happy to leave the issue for another generation, another day.

Or, as some people would say, 'Mañana.'

44   You Great Berk!

25th November

We have two theological students staying in our home for a whole month. The idea is to give them a feel of life 'on the other side'. In the middle of their years of learning theological theory, let them feel the frustration of not seeing one another except when parishioners are around! Let them discover how difficult it is to stick to time schedules when people arrive on the doorstep with pastoral emergencies.

They will have to write a report about us at the end of their time. I am a little anxious wondering whether Matthew's and my lifestyle will be open for judgement. Will it be too much of an eye-opener for them?

I am telling myself not to worry. They, too, are to be assessed – by Matthew. They probably feel as vulnerable as I do. And not entirely without reason, I might say. It is well known that students put their feet in it in all sorts of ways, and theological students are not exempt.

When Matthew was a student at college he worked for a month at a church in a really tough area in down-town

Nottingham. You name the problem, that estate had it; badly. Drugs, sexual abuse, child abuse, occult practices, poltergeists, debts, thieving, swindling, wife-battering. About half the men were in the nick. The one thing the parishioners did not have was inhibitions. Everyone knew about everyone else's devious ways.

When Matthew arrived on his first day he wasn't quite keyed into their way of doing things. He had had plenty of experience worshipping and helping in typical churches in 'nice' areas, but this really was something else.

The vicar, Carl, had grown up in a borstal himself, and had spent a couple of years in and out of prison until he was converted. He was a rough diamond with a very forthright manner. He seemed to view every conversation as an opportunity to get a knife into the backs of any 'Toffs', as he called them, who dogged the parishioners whom he loved.

On the first morning Carl sent Matthew off to visit a local family. The social worker had conveyed her concern since the school had reported bruises on one of the family's many children.

'Go and see the parents as a representative of the church,' Carl told Matthew. That was the only instruction Matthew received.

So along went Matthew, heart in mouth, to do his first ever official pastoral visit. A woman opened the door and she seemed pleased to have someone to chat to. She asked Matthew in for a cuppa. After an hour or so he left, feeling that he had done pretty well to have such a civil conversation without being shouted out.

He returned to the vicarage to meet with an inquisition.

'How did you get on?' asked Carl.

Matthew replied that he had had a friendly time.

'What about the kid?' pursued Carl, reaching for his tobacco tin. 'What did you say about him?'

'Well,' Matthew began, 'I sort of talked around the subject, and said very gently that things can get on top of you at times and when the strain gets too much she should ask for help, either from Social Services, or I reminded her that the church is here to help, too...'

Carl was not a man endowed with patience.

'You great berk!' he screamed. 'Idiot!' He completed rolling another cigarette and flicked the lighter noisily before he drew on the end strongly, as if he were drawing for strength to cope with yet another 'Toff' student.

Matthew was astonished and not a little put out. 'Why?' he asked.

'Did you think you'd give the woman a crossword to puzzle out or something?' With each angry word, smoke escaped from his mouth. 'Fancy talking round the subject like that!' He flicked his ash dismissively onto the floor.

Finally his rantings calmed and he became more positive. 'When she opened the door, you should have said, "God says bashing up your kids is wrong!" Then you go from there.'

There was no doubt, Matthew did become more direct in his approach from that student placement. He'll never forget how he learned.

I'm not sure that our present students will learn things in such a colourful way.

Vicars' Collections
45 (or, 100 Rings of Confidence)

2nd December

I went with Matthew last week to have breakfast with 100 clergy.

The host for this rather bizarre gathering was a well-known publisher who had very kindly slipped an extra invitation into Matthew's envelope for me to join with them. They had hoped this would provide an opportunity for them to discuss possibilities for a new writing project. With a mixture of feelings, from flattery to intrigue, I accepted.

What a vision at eight o'clock in the morning! The hotel dining room had ten circular tables, each adorned with ten grinning ministers. The early morning sunshine streaming through the elegant windows picked out the white of their dog collars: it was as if each one had a sparkling ring of confidence.

Matthew and I were introduced to the others already seated at our table. I was the only non-vicar there. At the mention of our names, one man beamed warmly.

'So *you're* Jane Grayshon,' he said, giving a firm

handshake. 'My wife and I enjoy hearing the high-jinks your family gets up to.' His reassuring smile conveyed an appreciation of my radio work which I valued. 'We listen to you every Sunday...'

The chap next to him, a younger man, chimed in. 'I don't,' he stated bluntly. 'I work on a Sunday morning.'

Was he suggesting he was different from all the other vicars, I wondered? His comment illustrated how insular some clergy can become.

The plates of bacon and egg, sausage and tomatoes arrived. As the buzz of conversation increased Matthew looked around and asked generally, 'What would you call a bunch of ministers all together? There must be one word for such a gathering.'

'Boring,' I suggested, but a sharp kick under the table told me to behave.

Matthew went on, 'I mean, it's not a herd, or a flock...'

'An assylum?' ventured the young vicar who works on Sundays.

'A communion?' came another, more helpfully.

'I think it should be a division,' said a lady deacon. I smiled at the helpful picture of an army division ready to fight for their cause: it would be good if clergy could be equally enthusiastic about their work. However, such a hope was rather shattered when she gave her reason: 'Clergy always seem to be divided.'

Her observation was a bit near the bone. The debate about women priests had already caused agonising division.

'How about a host?' One man clearly fancied a heavenly, angelic theme.

'Or a cloud?'

Hmm, yes, that fitted some of them, I mused. But I kept silent. I thought that those words made them all sound far too holy. Vicars aren't holy like that; not underneath. If you don't believe me, read the Bible. It says, 'All have sinned, and fall short of God's glory.'

By the time the coffee came round for the third time, the speech was beginning. At least, it was meant to be one speech, but actually there were three. The introduction extended to a long talk; similarly the thanks at the end.

This time it was the vicars who were on the receiving end of over-long talks. It was rather memorable that one vicar even fell asleep. When I say he 'fell' asleep, that is what I mean. He fell.

So, if you find you've had a little snooze during the sermon in your church one day, don't feel too guilty. Just quote Dick Fence.

46 Oh Jane, I Hope You Don't Kill Me

9th December

Life has had some peculiar moments since the television documentary was transmitted. I feel even more public property than I felt as 'just' the vicar's wife.

Last week our daughter Philippa was in hospital. Inevitably I spent a lot of time with her and I was amazed to watch the nurses' attitude towards me gradually change as they realised who I was.

It started when she was being admitted. 'Haven't I seen you somewhere before?' ventured the staff nurse writing out Philippa's nameband. We went through various possibilities until suddenly she remembered.

'I've seen you on TV!' she exclaimed.

And, equally suddenly, it was as if I became Someone to look at. Exhibit A.

It was exactly like when Matthew and I visited a different church. At the end of the service, three or four people made a bee-line towards us.

'Aren't you Jane Grayshon? The one who wrote those books?' or, 'The one from TV?'

I was tempted to say that the TV person was a half-hour extract from the life of a real person. But I had no time because, by then, they were turning to Matthew as well, asking if he was Jane Grayshon's husband; and I became too busy enjoying the fact that our roles had been reversed and I was no longer merely his wife.

One man asked Matthew in a rather confidential

tone, 'What's it like to be married to someone famous?'
What did they want him to say: that I pick my nose when
I think nobody's looking?

So, back on Philippa's ward, it was really quite a relief
when the ward sister took me to the canteen for a cup of
tea. I had come to know her a little when I was a patient
in the same hospital back in April.

'Jane,' she said rather solemnly, 'I've a confession to
make.'

I put on a relaxed-looking smile but inwardly I
steeled myself for whatever was to follow.

She said, 'It happened so quickly. I spoke before I
thought.' She bit her lip with regret. 'It was about you.'

I was intrigued. '*What* did you say?'

'Well, I was with a group of people when your name
came up. Several of them had read your books or heard
you speak. They started saying what a marvellous person you must be and I said, "I know her actually." They
went silent – sort of admiring – and I prayed God would
forgive me for my pride. And then they asked me what
you were like and ... Oh Jane, I hope you don't kill me.'

What could I say?

She went on, 'I told them, "Her tears are wet." That
got them puzzled so I added a bit more: "And they're
salty tears." They just sat there so I explained, "I knew
Jane when she was very ill and very distressed, and I saw
she's just the same as the rest of us."'

I cannot say too strongly what a relief it was for me to
hear that. It was a relief to be considered normal, to be
known as someone with human weaknesses instead of
someone with an unreachably high standard to live up
to.

I wonder if God wishes that more of us realised that
Jesus was so human that his tears were wet, and salty,
too.

And I am not alone, wriggling and squirming about

anyone thinking I'm different just because I'm vaguely 'famous'. Adrian Plass – who is a *really* famous author – wrote this month about a woman who had spoken pretty rudely to him just before he had addressed a meeting. At the end she had felt so dreadful for her mistake, she had apologised, 'I'm sorry, I just didn't know who you were earlier.'

Adrian's reply was very quiet: 'I'm the same person as I was when you didn't have time for me.'

47   The Vicar's Mistress

16th December

I am absolutely fed up with having a cold.

I don't know whether I've sounded croaky on the radio but for precisely eight weeks now I've been unable to talk properly. What started as a normal cough developed into a full-blown chest infection, until last week the doctor concluded I must have asthma.

'Asthma!' I mocked. 'I'd call it winter if you asked me. I need a good dose of warm sunshine to strip off to.'

And even with a new prescription I'm still left with catarrh and a bugged up dose.

They say one should look on the bright side; count one's blessings and all that. Well, so far I've only come up with one.

It occurred to me that because my voice sounds almost like someone else's, this situation has definite potential on the telephone. (You know how much that machine dominates my life.)

So... Wednesday. Having come back from the doctor, I felt really fed up. And the phone rang.

'This is your moment, Grayshon,' I told myself.

This is true, by the way.

Emphasising the nasal bit to sound as Scouse as I could I picked it up, saying, "Ello, Sainte Mark's Vic'ridge.'

The chap at the other end asked who I was. Without the least trace of hesitation I said, 'I'm the cook for the vic'ridge.'

That mystified him. I hoped it wasn't the bishop, or someone in dire need. I'm not sure which would have been worse. But it didn't sound like either. This guy just asked, 'I'm sorry?'

I said, 'Yerr, I'm sorry too. Specially cos I don't get paid for it.'

Then, since he obviously didn't know how to respond, I went on, 'Didn't you know this vicar's gorr a cook, then?'

I could almost hear the poor man shuffling dubiously. 'As a matter of fact I thought that his wife cooked. Is she not well again, then?'

I didn't think it was fair to keep it up any longer. I explained that this was his wife, and sometimes a vicar's wife feels like a mere cook and secretary, unpaid, and that yes, I was unwell with a bad cold but women just keep going anyway, and could I help *him*?

It was a brief phone call.

A bit naughty really. I mean, the way we live is supposed to reflect God, and he never hides who he is. In fact, one of the nice things about God is that he makes himself known to us when we're not even expecting him to.

There was one occasion when I made my position known to a lady at our church when she definitely wasn't expecting it. It was at the end of the service while we were all having a cup of coffee. Trying to welcome someone I didn't know, I began to make general conversation.

She asked which area of town I live in, and she almost gasped at my reply. In a rather awed voice she asked, 'Isn't that where the vicar lives?'

'That's right,' I said.

'Doesn't he live on such-and-such a road?' she asked, as if the matter were entirely confidential.

'That's right,' I said. 'I live on the same road.'

She seemed impressed. And I'm not sure quite what happened next, but I think that my mischievous nature rather got the better of me.

Mimicking her hushed tone, I leaned towards her and said, 'In fact, I've been to bed with the vicar.'

She looked so shocked. She turned in dismay and scanned around those nearby lest I'd been overheard. I later learned that she was checking that the lady she had assumed to be the vicar's wife was well out of earshot.

I had to put her out of her misery. 'I am his wife,' I grinned.

Relief swept over her like a wave. She had thought I was his mistress.

Isn't the vicar's wife allowed to be his mistress as well?

48

Shoulders back, Bottom in, Bust out, Tummy in

23rd December

Is it just me, or does everybody find it hard to stick to being their simple selves when they're surrounded by overpowering people?

Matthew and I often get invited to official functions in the community, especially around Christmas-time when people want to give a formal nod to the church. Oh, some people at such dos can be oppressive! And although I know God wants each of us to be content as we are, I do not enjoy feeling squashed by others who seem pretentious and harsh.

I once represented Matthew and myself at such a gathering at a College of Further Education. The invitation had been for lunch with the principal, staff, and certain 'visitors' to the college.

I did not know beforehand, but the Home Economics students were being judged for some national cookery competition. When I ambled up to the principal's office,

instead of finding just a few folk as I had imagined, the place was buzzing.

It was all frightfully far back dahling; the room was already heavy with the stink of rich perfume mixed with cigar smoke – yuk. I didn't recognise a soul. I wished that Matthew had made time to come. He would have helped me to keep my hair on.

Oh well, you're here now, I thought. Just be yourself, Jane.

I took a deep breath. Shoulders back, bottom in, bust out, tummy in (I'd been taught all that at school) and I entered, accepting my sherry gratefully.

I tried ever so hard not to join in their accents. Matthew always says he knows who I'm speaking to on the telephone by how my accent changes, and I did hear myself drop into a few 'Oh no, how ghastly!'s. But that was more to practise imitating them than anything else. Mostly I reckoned I was just being me.

Then it was announced that we were all to 'view the display of award-winning gâteaux' (pronounced with emphasis on the last syllable) and everyone made their way – graciously of course – to the stairs. I found myself walking next to a woman I had not met.

Now sometimes you meet a person who's a Someone, and the worst bit about this occasion was that I didn't have a clue who she was.

She said, 'I'm *so* glad to have the opportunity to see other people's creativity. Cake decorating is just not my forte.'

She sounded more out of her depth than I was, so I joked, 'Ooh, I'm glad to meet another pleb cook like myself.'

She seemed to hesitate a little on the stairs, before extending her hand towards me.

'I'm Marguerite Patten,' she said.

I could feel myself shrivel up. I hovered at the edge of

the next step. There I was, eyeball to eyeball with this world-famous cook, and I had had the temerity to address her as a 'pleb cook like myself'. My mind swam with apologies. But how on earth was I to have known who she was? No more than she knew who I was.

Come to think of it, she hadn't asked anything about me.

Forcing myself to sound as relaxed and confident as the books claim is essential, I reciprocated her hand-shake and replied, 'And I'm Jane Grayshon.'

I let my smile convey quite simply that God loves her AND me, the same.

At least, I hope it did.

49   The Vicar's Wife's Husband

30th December

There's one big drawback with these broadcasts.

I started off telling you how I *hate* being referred to as 'the vicar's wife'.

In fact I've still got the script of the very first episode, and I can quote to you my actual words. I said, 'I *never* introduce myself as a vicar's wife.... It's infuriating!'

That hasn't changed. I cannot describe how strongly I loathe that sort of introduction. You see, it puts me in a box. It makes everyone expect me to be a stuffy old boring humourless frump.

That makes me want to step out and sometimes – I must confess – the only way I can think of doing so is by saying something which will shock. I try to shock only enough to make people sit up and think, and realise that not all vicars' wives are stuffy old boring humourless frumps.

That's why I've spent week after week this year trying to share a little of what life's like for us supposedly-angelic creatures. Trying to describe what goes on on the *other* side of the vicarage front door.

Well, you know what's happened now, don't you? It's had exactly the opposite effect from what I intended. I'm referred to as a vicar's wife far more often than ever before.

I suppose it's my own fault. It's as if I've put a nail in my own coffin (although I shouldn't use that phrase at home, because being a vicarage there may be a visiting undertaker around, who might take me literally).

And this programme has affected my husband, too. Apart from the fact that it's ruined any chances for promotion, or so I'm told, he also gets introduced in very peculiar ways nowadays.

Like the time he went recently to visit a parishioner in our local hospital. Another patient saw the dog collar and called out, 'Hang on a minute!'

Matthew went over to the chap's bedside, thinking he maybe wanted a deep and meaningful conversation.

Very seriously, the patient asked, 'Where are you from?'

'Runcorn,' replied Matthew.

'Oh, I wondered.' He seemed interested. 'There's a vicar from Runcorn who's got a vicar's wife on radio...'

Matthew was eager to reply then. 'Yes, I'm that vicar's wife's husband.'

What a job description! The vicar's wife's husband. What a poor, depersonalised man my husband must be. Nobody even wanted his autograph, they were having such a good chuckle about the Confessions of the vicar's wife.

I think it's a good job he has a strong conviction that he's doing what God wants him to do. It's a conviction we'd all like, I guess deep down.

But, having made my own confessions here for fifty-two weeks, it's time for me to stop. This is not the end:

I'm just completing the book, the written version of *The Confessions of the Vicar's Wife*, which is due to be published next March (so long as I get it to the publisher in the next three weeks).

I know there are some people who will be delighted to hear I'm taking a break; people who stop in mid-sentence and say, 'I've got an awful feeling I'm going to get quoted.'

Or those who, when they hear me answer the telephone, say, 'Oh, er, I hesitate to phone you...'

Mind you, I wish a few more people would hesitate, at least long enough to consider the time of their call. I mean, last week the phone rang at 7.55 in the morning with an enquiry about a meeting. I knew nothing about it and suggested that the person phone the leader of that meeting.

'Oooh no, I couldn't do that,' she said.

'Why not?' I asked.

'Not at this time in the morning. I couldn't phone anyone at this time in the morning.'

I left a pause so she could maybe listen to what she'd just said. But as she didn't seem to have heard herself I reflected, 'You're phoning me.'

Her reply came without hesitation. 'That's different,' she said.

I yet have to discover what is so different about being a vicar's wife.

I hope I never do.

The Maestro

by T Davis Bunn

Giovanni di Alta – Gianni – is an Italian-American raised by his grandmother in Dusseldorf. A musician of outstanding ability, he trains as a classical guitarist, but breaks away from the austere discipline in search of the warmer, more fluid worlds of rock and jazz.

His mounting fame and wealth, the drugs and the beautiful women, do not reach his inner emptiness. Wounds inflicted by his mother's death and his father's subsequent rejection bring him to the sharp edge of despair.

But not for ever. The regeneration of Giovanni di Alta is about to begin – and from a very unexpected source.

This deeply satisfying, carefully crafted novel will hang in the mind long after the book is finished.

T. Davis Bunn and his wife Isabella, both Americans, currently live in Henley on Thames.

£4.99 from Monarch Publications   *400 pp*

Vienna Prelude

by Bodie Thoene

Predating the events of the Zion Chronicles series, *Vienna Prelude* opens in pre-World War II Austria. Elisa Lindheim, a violinist with the Vienna Symphony Orchestra, is of Jewish heritage but has adopted an Aryan stage name. Thus she is able to travel and play in Germany, even though a 1935 law forbade Jewish musicians to do so. Her dear friends, Leah, a cellist, and Leah's husband Shimon, must escape Austria or perish in the coming Holocaust.

John Murphy, a reporter for the New York Times in Berlin and Austria, becomes linked with English politicians in a plan to overthrow Hitler. Elisa and John's mutual connections with the Jewish Underground entangle them in a web of intrigue, danger and conspiracy – which is aggravated by their own complex relationship.

The saga unfolds further in *Prague Counterpoint*.

£4.99 from Monarch Publications *416 pp*

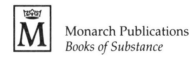 Monarch Publications
Books of Substance

All Monarch books can be purchased from your local general or Christian bookshop. In case of difficulty, they may be ordered from the publisher:

Monarch Publications
P O Box 163
Tunbridge Wells
Kent
TN3 0NZ

Please enclose a cheque payable to Monarch Publications for the cover price plus 60p for the first book ordered plus 40p per copy for each additional book ordered to a maximum charge of £3.00 to cover postage and packing (UK and Republic of Ireland only).

Overseas customers please order from:

Christian Marketing PTY Ltd
P O Box 154
Victoria 3215
Australia

Omega Distributors Ltd
69 Great South Road
Remuera
Auckland
New Zealand

Struik Christian Books
P O Box 193
Maitland 7405
Cape Town
South Africa

Kingsway USA Inc
4717 Hunter's Crossing Drive
Old Hickory
TN 37138
USA

Christian Marketing Canada
P O Box 7000
Niagara-on-the-Lake
Ontario L0S 1J0
Canada